A Place for You

by Mark Spellman

Living
Legacy
PUBLISHING

Dedication

This book is dedicated to my family. First, to my beloved wife, Kimberly, who has made the last 28 years of my life so fulfilling, joyful, adventurous, and exciting. You have been a very loving, consistent, and powerful wind in my sails. You are crowned in His glory, and you are full of beauty!

To my two awesome sons, Samuel, and Daniel, I am eternally thankful that God brought you into my life. Your place in my heart and in my life is a place that only God could have given.

You all are truly a gift from God! Each of you have taught my heart as a husband and father to really taste of an eternal Love. To each of you, I say THANK YOU!

Establishing and Equipping Kingdom Minded People & Families

#FamilyMission

Family Mission is a Kingdom Work
focusing on a **Divine Reset**
of the Mission of God's Royal Family.

A great SHIFT occurs when we allow
the Word of God and Holy Spirit to
reset God's original Kingdom plan
for Man and His Royal Family.

**The Blood of Jesus was shed to
redeem and release
your Destiny and His Legacy.**

"Heal the Home and Heal the Land!"

The 7 Mission Objectives of the Family Mission Mandate

Mission Objective 1

<u>Family Mission</u> is working to help everyone experience a **<u>DIVINE RESET</u>** so they can fulfill their God-given destiny as a part of His legacy. "And by the blood of His cross, everything in heaven and earth is **brought back to Himself— back to its original intent, restored to innocence again!**" (Colossians 1:20 TPT) Jesus said if you make the tree good the fruit will be good (Matthew 12:33). Family Mission is working to help everyone understand and embrace their TRUE and ORIGINAL value, identity, and purpose - what it truly means to be BORN-AGAIN. When we understand OUR DIVINE NATURE in Christ and the WHY behind our lives, we will make every day a WIN!

Mission Objective 2

Family Mission is working to **REVIVE THE MISSION OF LOVE** [which is the mission of family]. Every home can be: A Mission Base, A Lighthouse, and An Embassy in the Kingdom of God. The revelation of the cross will establish an altar in every home. The Mission of Love is what Jesus was talking about when He said to take up **the cross** and follow Him (Mark 10:21). He was telling us to take up **the Mission of Love** and live like He lived! E. W. Kenyon said, "The genius of Christianity is the ability of God to build Himself into us through His Word so that in our everyday life we live like the Master." **Just like with Joseph, God desires to live and love through all of us to bring about a great deliverance!**

Mission Objective 3

Family Mission is working to keep **WORSHIP** in the CONTEXT of family. The word *worship* is first used in Genesis 22. Here we see **a covenant family working together in covenant love, fulfilling a covenant Kingdom purpose**, and working with God and each other to fulfill a redemptive purpose in the Family of God. **Jesus Himself put worship in the context of the family** when He spoke of the Father's desire for WORSHIP! Our Father is not seeking true worshippers for validation and affirmation. He is seeking true worshippers for **intimacy, agreement, and partnership** in His plans and purposes. Intimacy, agreement, and partnership are the high calling of marriage and family!

Mission Objective 4

<u>Family Mission</u> is working to help everyone move in and experience their **MANSION RIGHT NOW.** Jesus said, "I go to prepare a place for you," (John 14:2,23). Jesus prepared a place for us in Him and in the Father: **a place for Him and the Father in us**. When we understand the power and wisdom of A SEED, the Kingdom of God is opened to us in all its glory (John 12:23-28). **"I pray that everyone who meets you would catch your faith and learn how wonderful it is to LIVE IN CHRIST JE-SUS!"** (Philemon 6, Laubach Translation)

Mission Objective 5

<u>Family Mission</u> Our work is focused on **FAMILY** so that a Glorious Church can fully rise up. Paul referred to a Glorious Church in Ephesians 5:27. The Holy Spirit intentionally nestled this revelation amid His instructions for MARRIAGE and FAMILY. It's scripturally unreasonable to think a Glorious Church will fully rise up without making marriage and family all that God originally intended them to be. Marriage and family are called to be powerful witnesses of Christ and His relationship with the Church. The richest application of any revelation in scripture is always in its CONTEXT.

Mission Objective 6

Family Mission is working in **PRAYER**. Prayer is working with the Father, Holy Spirit, and Jesus, and all of Them with us as described in John 17. Jesus was extremely effective and intentional in prayer, and we should be too. In John 17 He said the words, "THAT THEY..." 10 times and that's no accident! The word *that* **expresses consequence, result, or effect.** Prayer changes radically when we understand we're not just praying to God but working WITH HIM in prayer. Our **intimacy**, **agreement,** and **partnership** are vital to Him and to us. Nothing can separate us from the love of God, so nothing can separate us from working with God in prayer.

Mission Objective 7

<u>Family Mission</u> has a passion that burns for **ALL NATIONS.** People of **every nation**, tribe, and tongue deserve a chance to experience a DIVINE RESET and be BORN AGAIN. We want everyone to have the opportunity to embrace their God-given DESTINY as a part of His Family and LEGACY!

The Kingdom Work of Family Mission is a multigenerational mandate! We will use every available platform to teach, train, equip, and mentor. This includes the use of meetings, conferences, retreats, books, workbooks, the internet, media, podcasts, etc. We are working to establish Mission Bases and Fellowships in the United States. We joyfully travel to congregations in the United States as well as host a variety of events. **The Multigenerational Mandate of Family Mission will be taken to the Nations as the Lord directs.**

Family Mission Recognizes
the 7 Mountains of Influence

Education … Faith … Family … Business … Government … Arts & Entertainment … Media

Table of Contents

Introduction

A Place for You was written for you under a Heavenly Mandate. It's the Mandate of Family Mission. Our Heavenly Father's Mission was about a family from the beginning, and it will be about a family throughout all eternity. This book assignment has been **bathed in much prayer and intercession,** just like Queen Esther of old who prepared herself for one night with the King. That one night changed everything and brought about a great deliverance. I believe this book will help you take your place in history with a plan and purpose that you're destined to. Scripture says Esther was born for such a time as this, and so are YOU.

I believe that about your life. You were born for such a time as this. Scripture says there is a time to be born and here you are! The anointing and fragrance upon this book will create a Divine Shift and a Divine Reset in your thinking and your life! This book is a living coal taken from the altar in Heaven. It contains fire and revelation from Heaven. Let it touch your life. Let it touch your lips. After you're finished reading *A Place for You*, like Isaiah, you will be saying, **"Here am I, Lord, send me!"**

Proverbs says, "Wisdom is the principal thing. In all your getting get understanding," (4:7). This book is all about getting wisdom, understanding, and knowledge from Heaven. It's eternal wisdom, understanding, and knowledge. Eternal wisdom is the ancient landmark established by God in the book of beginnings, Genesis! This is what Jesus came to re-establish in the heart of man and the family of God!

> *"Through wisdom a house is **built**, And by understanding it is **established**; By knowledge the rooms are **filled** With all precious and pleasant riches."*

Proverbs 24:3-4 NKJV

> *"Through skillful and godly Wisdom is a house **(a life, a home, a family)** built, and by understanding it is established [on a sound and good foundation], And by knowledge shall its chambers [of every area] be filled with all precious and pleasant riches."*

Proverbs 24:3-4 AMPC

Introduction

My intention in writing this book is to both reset and build your life, home, and family with the eternal wisdom of God. I want your life, home, and family built upon a sound and good foundation. Storms come to everyone. Having your house on the solid foundation of Christ is the key to winning and thriving in every season of life. If for any reason you are not sure if you're born-again or you've never been baptized in the Holy Spirit and Fire, then there are two prayers in Appendix 1 that I would encourage you to turn to and pray once you finish with this introduction. Appendix 1 is there as a resource for you to lead others in prayer as well.

> *"Wise people are builders — they build families, businesses, communities. And through intelligence and insight their enterprises are established and endure. Because of their skilled leadership, the hearts of people are filled with the treasures of wisdom and the pleasures of spiritual wealth. Wisdom can make anyone into a mighty warrior, and revelation-knowledge increases strength.* **Wise strategy is necessary to wage war, and with many astute advisers you'll see the path to victory more clearly."**
>
> **Proverbs 24:3-6 TPT**

I believe the eternal strategy, wisdom, understanding, and knowledge released in this book will help you see the path to victory more clearly in every circumstance and season of life! We must have Heaven's perspective. Psalm 139 will beautifully prepare your heart for the precious seeds that will be sown and watered in your heart as you read *A Place for You*. Please read the Psalm below slowly and prayerfully.

"Lord, you know everything there is to know about me. You perceive every movement of my heart and soul, and you understand my every thought before it even enters my mind. You are so intimately aware of me, Lord. You read my heart like an open book, and you know all the words I'm about to speak before I even start a sentence! You know every step I will take before my journey even begins. You have gone into my future to prepare the way, and in kindness you follow behind me to spare me from the harm of my past. You have laid your hand on me! This is just too wonderful, deep, and incomprehensible! Your understanding of me brings me wonder and strength.

Where could I go from your Spirit? Where could I run and hide from your face? If I go up to heaven, you're there! If I go down to the realm of the dead, you're there too! If I fly with wings into the shining dawn, you're there!

Introduction

If I fly into the radiant sunset, you're there waiting! Wherever I go, your hand will guide me; your strength will empower me. It's impossible to disappear from you or to ask the darkness to hide me, for your presence is everywhere, bringing light into my night. There is no such thing as darkness with you. The night, to you, is as bright as the day; there's no difference between the two.

You formed my innermost being, shaping my delicate inside and my intricate outside, and wove them all together in my mother's womb. I thank you, God, for making me so mysteriously complex! Everything you do is marvelously breathtaking. It simply amazes me to think about it! How thoroughly you know me, Lord!

You even formed every bone in my body when you created me in the secret place; carefully, skillfully you shaped me from nothing to something. You saw who you created me to be before I became me! Before I'd ever seen the light of day, the number of days you planned for me were already recorded in your book.

Every single moment you are thinking of me! How precious and wonderful to consider that you cherish me constantly in your every thought! O God, your desires toward me are more than the grains of sand on every shore! When I awake each morning, you're still with me.

God, I invite your searching gaze into my heart. Examine me through and through; find out everything that may be hidden within me. Put me to the test and sift through all my anxious cares. See if there is any path of pain I'm walking on, and lead me back to your glorious, everlasting way— the path that brings me back to you."

Psalms 139:1-18, 23-24 TPT

The Blood of Jesus was shed to Redeem and Release your Destiny and His Legacy!

CHAPTER ONE

What is Truth?

Life is full of questions. Life has plenty of mysteries. From the day you are born you're on a road of discovery. Along the way you will constantly come across things and go through stuff that will leave you wondering. You will find yourself asking the questions why or how come? Questions are not bad at all. The issue is, do you really want the answer? Do you really want the truth? I did not say **an** answer. I said **the** answer. When Jesus stood before the Roman Governor Pilate just before He was to be crucified, He was asked a very important question.

"Pilate asked Him, 'Are you a King?' Jesus answered, 'My Kingdom is not of this world...' Pilate said, 'Are you a King then?'" Jesus answered with something EXTREME-LY important here. "You say rightly that I am a king. For this cause, I was born, and for this cause I have come into the world, **that I should bear witness to the truth**. Everyone who is of **the truth** hears My voice." Listen now to Pilate's response; he cried out, "WHAT IS TRUTH?" (John 18:36-38).

What is Truth?

What is truth? This, my brother, and my sister, is truly the million-dollar question! This is the question you better get answered before you depart this life! **What is truth?** I believe this is the question in every soul trying to find their way through life, no matter what continent you live on or what language you may speak. Many times, people will not phrase it that way, but still, it is the question deep down in their hearts. Ecclesiastes 3:11 declares a sense of eternity in every person's heart! Jesus is the Truth. Jesus is the Life. Jesus is the Way! (John 14:6)

The Apostle Paul, after his conversion on the road to Damascus, received the revelation of the Gospel, but he did not receive it from any man. He received it by a direct REVELATION OF JESUS CHRIST HIMSELF! (Gal. 1:11,12) Paul was used by God to write the majority of the New Testament. It is very interesting to see how many times he refers to his revelation knowledge as the "revealing of a mystery," or the "understanding of a mystery."

What is Truth?

When you think about a mystery, you think about something hidden or about discovering and solving something. This is important to understand. God did not hide things **from** you, He has hidden things **for** you. Truth is hidden and is **fully intended to be found by those who want the Truth.** God even gave us the treasure map. That's exactly what the Bible is. It's a treasure map to discover the Truth!

The truth about who God is.

The truth about who man is.

The truth about who YOU are.

It's a treasure map that helps you discover the truth regarding the meaning of life and the meaning of your existence. The Apostle Paul found the Truth. Or it could be said, the Truth found him! I will discuss more about this dynamic of who found whom later in this book.

As we begin our journey together let's take some time and consider a few of the scriptures where Paul speaks of the mystery he discovered. These are not all the scriptures that could be referenced, but certainly, enough for you to embark on your great quest. A quest where you discover the mystery of the ages. A quest where you discover and come alive in all the light that was released in the life of Christ! I am going to reference twelve examples from

Paul's writings and three from Jesus in the Gospels regarding the mystery of the ages.

Remember what Jesus said to Pilate! "Everyone who is of the truth will hear my voice." That means everyone who wants **the truth** (not a truth) will find Jesus. Period! If someone wants **THE TRUTH**, they will find Jesus Christ! He promised they would hear His voice. Therefore, learning to hear His voice is the most important thing you could learn in this life.

Example One

*"But we speak the wisdom of God in a **mystery**, the **hidden wisdom** which God ordained before the ages for our glory, which none of the rulers of this age knew; for had they known, they would not have crucified the Lord of glory."*

1 Corinthians 2:7–8

Notice this mystery has been ordained for God's glory in your life. God ordained that you would receive, understand, and express His glory! No wonder the rulers of this age regretted crucifying Jesus, the Lord of glory. Jesus, by planting His life, released the glory in His life. The seed of the glorious Gospel is now seeding the hearts of people everywhere around the world. The Bible teaches that you are born again when that glorious seed of the Gospel is planted in your heart by faith. You will also share and release His glory by planting your life into the Mission of Love! Taking up your cross and following Him is taking up the Mission of Love!

Example Two

*"Let a man so consider us, as servants of Christ and **stewards of the mysteries of God.** Moreover, it is required in stewards that one be found faithful."*

1 Corinthians 4:1–2

Scripture reveals that you and I will give an account of the stewardship of our lives. You might be thinking, "Don't put that pressure on me!" Yet the Word of God teaches that we are accountable to the One who created us and redeemed us. We will all give an account for our lives at the judgment seat of Christ (II Corinthians 5:10). The judgment seat of Christ is not about whether you go to Heaven or not. Where you spend eternity is determined by what family you're in. This is why faith in the blood of Jesus is so important! Those who have put faith in Christ for their salvation have had all their sins washed away by the blood of Jesus. Unfortunately, many people serve a God they've created in their minds and are not really communicating with the God of the Bible, the God, and Father of our Lord Jesus Christ.

Accountability is a good thing. The judgment seat of Christ is about how you live out your life in the ages to come. It's what you do in this life that will determine what work, responsibilities, privileges, and rewards you will have in and throughout the ages to come! Please let that sink in. The reason for the judgment seat of Christ is to determine rewards! That's right - rewards! God is a rewarder. God wants to reward your faithfulness, and He's going to be JUST in His rewards. God is not a socialist or a communist just spreading the wealth around. Ephesians 2:7 says, *"that in the ages to come He might show the exceeding riches of His grace in His kindness toward us in Christ Jesus."* Glory to God!

Example Three

> ***"The mystery*** *which has been hidden from ages and from generations, but now has been revealed to His saints. To them, God willed to make known what the riches of the glory of this mystery among the Gentiles are: which is Christ in you, the hope of glory."*
>
> **Colossians 1:26–27**

What is Truth?

God desires to reveal the mystery! He wants you to find the Truth. He wants you to experience the Truth. **He wants Christ in You!** This is a huge part of the mystery. This is what the devil regrets so much. He thought he killed Jesus, but suddenly Christ came alive again in the Church! Now there are Anointed Ones (Christians) alive everywhere. Therefore, our adversary tries to keep this mystery hidden. The devil doesn't mind if you go to church or simply know **about** God. What he cannot afford is for Christians to discover that they are Anointed Ones as well, that Christ is in them. No, you're not the redeemer of humanity, but you are anointed and working with God's redemptive purpose for today. That is the Mission of Love. You have the anointing in you and upon you! In you at the new birth and upon you at the baptism of the Holy Spirit.

You are the temple of the Holy Spirit! (II Corinthians 6:14-18) That's what the word *Christian* means. I like to say it this way, we are In-Christ-Ones! Anointed Ones. Glory to God! It takes humility and trust to walk in the truth of scripture. The truth does not feed your ego, and it will definitely keep you on your knees.

Paul says in Colossians 1:27 that it's Christ in you that is the hope of glory. The word *hope* here is biblically defined as "joyful, confident expectation." Unfortunately, this is not the way most people use the word *hope*. Most use the word *hope* like they use the word *wish*. When most people say, "I hope so" they are really saying, "I wish it would happen."

As In-Christ-Ones you get to live in the joyful expectation, or hope, of the glory of God! If the privilege of being the expression of the glory of God doesn't give you joy, then what will? This truth of Christ in us, the hope of glory, is a source of continuous joy! It's a joy that never fades or diminishes. If a Christian has lost their joy, it's because they have forgotten Christ is in them. They forgot about the privilege of revealing the glory of God! Nothing else is required to walk in CONSTANT JOY! Access to CONSTANT JOY is an amazing reality. This is what the Passion Translation calls the astonishing revelation of the Gospel. Look at some of these key scriptures found in Colossians chapter 1 (TPT).

The Astonishing Revelation of the Gospel

"This is the wonderful message that is being spread everywhere, powerfully changing hearts throughout the earth, just like it has changed you! Every believer of this good news bears the fruit of eternal life as they experience the reality of God's grace. Our beloved coworker,

*Epaphras, was there from the beginning to thoroughly teach you **the astonishing revelation of the Gospel,** and he serves you faithfully as Christ's representative."*

Verses 6-7

*Your hearts can soar with joyful gratitude when you think of how God made you worthy to receive the glorious inheritance freely given to us by living in the light. He has rescued us completely from the tyrannical rule of darkness and has translated us into the kingdom realm of his beloved Son. **For in the Son all our sins are canceled, and we have the release of redemption through his very blood.***"

Verses 12-14

*"**And by the blood of his cross, everything in heaven and earth is brought back to himself—back to its original intent, restored to innocence again!** Even though you were once distant from him, living in the shadows of your evil thoughts and actions, he reconnected you back to himself. He released his supernatural peace to you through the sacrifice of his own body as the sin-payment on your behalf so that*

you would dwell in his presence. And now there is nothing between you and Father God, for he sees you as holy, flawless, and restored, if indeed you continue to advance in faith, assured of a firm foundation to grow upon. Never be shaken from the hope of the Gospel you have believed in. ***And this is the glorious news I preach all over the world."***

Verses 20-23

"There is a divine mystery—a secret surprise *that has been concealed from the world for generations, but now it's being revealed, unfolded and manifested for every holy believer to experience. Living within you is the Christ who floods you with the expectation of glory!* ***This mystery of Christ, embedded within us,*** *becomes a heavenly treasure chest of hope filled with the riches of glory for his people, and God wants everyone to know it."*

Verses 26-27

*"****Christ is our message! We preach to awaken hearts and bring every person into the full understanding of truth.*** *It has become my inspiration and passion in ministry to labor*

with a tireless intensity, with his power flow-ing through me, **to present to every believer the revelation of being his perfect one in Jesus Christ.***"*

Verses 28-29

Christ is in you! You are a heavenly treasure chest of hope filled with the riches of the glory of God. Expect the glory of God! Romans 15:13 says that your joy and peace is connected to your believing and not to your circumstances. It also connects your joy to the God of hope! *"Now may the God of hope fill you with all joy and peace in believing, that you may abound in hope by the power of the Holy Spirit,"* (Romans 15:13).

Example Four

"For I want you to know what a great conflict I have for you and those in Laodicea, and for as many as have not seen my face in the flesh, that their hearts may be encouraged, being knit to-gether in love, and attaining to all riches of the full assurance of understanding, to the knowl-edge of **the mystery of God***, both of the Father and of Christ, in whom are* **hidden** *all the trea-sures of wisdom and knowledge."*

Colossians 2:1–3

Now this is just getting more and more overwhelming! You have access to all the treasures of wisdom and knowledge! ALL THE TREASURES OF WISDOM AND KNOWLEDGE! What? I like to say it this way. The Word of God is not just meant for your head, it's meant for your spirit! Your finite mind can only contain so much, but your spirit has the capacity to receive the full truth of the Word of God. One of the best things you and I can do is to pray in the spirit (with other tongues) and ask the Holy Spirit to reveal the truth to us and in us! Praying in the spirit helps to keep the river of God flowing in your life. According to Jude's epistle it helps keep you in the love of God (Jude 20,21). Notice again in the text above that **our being knit together in love** leads to attaining to all the riches of the full assurance of understanding! Truth and love are inseparable. I want to say it again: **Truth and love are inseparable!** Ephesians 4:15 says the truth is to be communicated in love!

Example Five

> *"Meanwhile praying also for us, that God would open to us a door for the word, to speak **the mystery of Christ**, for which I am also in chains, that I may make it manifest, as I ought to speak"*

Colossians 4:3–4

If you're going to truly communicate the truth, you must have a door opened in the spirit. This means you and I are going to have to pave the way in prayer. It's important for you and I to be praying for the people we are communicating with on a regular basis. Praying for people when we know that we will have the opportunity to speak to them will invite God into the conversation. Spiritual understanding and knowledge are not just about intellect and information. Much prayer has gone into this book and much prayer continues over every reader. Since you have this book in your hands, you have been prayed for and are being prayed for. I'm expecting you to fully come alive in love and in the Truth. I pray you will be the express image of His glory everyday of your life!

Doors are important. Doors mean access, and if they're open, they often mean permission. If we are going to speak into someone's life, then we need access and we need permission. Just because I am speaking to my wife, or she is speaking to me does not guarantee we are communicating. Many times, husbands and wives have walls up inside their heart and filters over their ears. This is true of everyone. I like the famous saying, "People do not care what you know until they know that you care!" So, an open door to communicate is actually an invisible door, but it is a very real thing. We will talk more about this later in this book but know that all communication ceases in a threatening environment. As communicators we have to work to remove the threat if we are going to understand one another. It doesn't matter if the threat is real or perceived; it needs to be removed. The cross of Jesus Christ removed the threat so that open communication could be experienced by all of God's children who are washed in the blood of Jesus. The grace and faith we express towards people will go a long way to remove the threat or open the door for true communication.

Example Six

"In Him we have redemption through His blood, the forgiveness of sins, according to the riches of His grace which He made to abound toward us in all wisdom and prudence, having made known to us **the mystery of His will,** *according to His good pleasure which He purposed in Himself, that in the dispensation of the fullness of the times He might gather together in one all things in Christ, both which are in heaven and which are on earth—in Him."*

Ephesians 1:7–10

What is Truth?

God wants you to know His will and the plan He has for your life. He did not hide it **from** you, He hid it **for** you! God has ordained you to know His will and His plan for your life. The scripture above says that God's plan involves "the fullness of times." It involves Him gathering together all things in one. When we talk about His will, we're not just talking about whether or not you're supposed to be a plumber or an architect. It's not just whether or not you're supposed to be a nurse or a movie actor. Yes, God has those things planned for our lives, but the most important issue is **what are you becoming?** What is your identity? What is the "why" behind your life? What is the reason you were given life? What is your perspective on life? What is your motive in life?

Regardless of what your hands find to do, regardless of what your talents and gifts and skills are, they are all to serve the mission of love! It's often easy to get tunnel vision, thinking this life is all there is. No, God is completely outside the boundaries of time. This is why He was able to have the wisdom and ability to send His Son and reset the plan for His family, a family that was separated from Him in the Garden of Eden. There is a plan for His family. You're not just going to sit on clouds and play harps forever. This life is really just testing, preparing, and qualifying you for where and how you will work with Him throughout the ages to come.

When you keep an eternal perspective, you keep life in a healthy perspective. God is a God of legacy. Your destiny is tied to His legacy. Later in this book we're going to talk about Abraham. God is known throughout scripture as the God of Abraham, Isaac, and Jacob. He is always thinking generationally. He always has legacy in mind. I want to say it again, your destiny is irrevocably tied to His legacy. If you're going to fully grasp the impact and meaning of the mystery, then you too need to think generationally and in line with legacy. Oh, what a glorious truth, that we are a part of His legacy!

Please don't **let that be a small thing in your eyes.** You may want to go out the next few nights and do like God told Abraham. Look up in the night sky and just imagine. Consider the stars of the heavens! Consider His love for you and His investment in your life. You were worth the blood of Jesus! Consider that your life is no accident, and He has a purpose for it.

Like Jeremiah, before you were in your mother's womb, He knew you and ordained you! (Jeremiah 1:5) You do not have to understand all the implications of this, but you do need to connect with it. You need to believe it and expect Holy Spirit to lead you and guide you in understanding it. This is why God paid such a high price for your life! He has a plan for your life that is way beyond your few short years here on earth. Even if you lived to be 120 years old, that's just a few years in light of living eternally. This is all directly connected with you accepting the identity of love and the Mission of Love!

Example Seven

*"For this reason I, Paul, the prisoner of Christ Jesus for you Gentiles— if indeed you have heard of the dispensation of the grace of God which was given to me for you, how that by revelation He made known to me **the mystery** (as I have briefly written already, by which, when you read, you may understand my knowledge in **the mystery of Christ**), which in other ages was not made known to the sons of men, as it has now been revealed by the Spirit to His holy apostles and prophets: that the Gentiles should be fellow heirs, of the same body, and partakers of His promise in Christ through the Gospel...To me, who am less than the least of all the saints, this grace was given, that I should preach among the Gentiles the unsearchable riches of Christ, and to make all see what is **the fellowship of the mystery**, which from the*

beginning of the ages has been hidden in God who created all things through Jesus Christ;"

Ephesians 3:1–6,8,9

One of the greatest joys in life is having fellowship with other believers about the mysteries of the Gospel. Talking with people whose lives have been transformed by the Gospel is a powerful thing. There's also great joy in sharing the Gospel with others who may not believe or may not have ever heard it. Many people have questions about life. They feel like life is a great mystery. When you have a grasp on the truth, you can minister to them and reveal to them the mystery of life. Your voice can actually contain the love and voice of Jesus to them. The Holy Spirit works with you to reveal Christ and the Mission of Love to them. Acts 1:8 says you're anointed to give witness and testimony concerning Jesus. Psalm 107:2 in the NIV says, "Let the redeemed of the Lord tell their story." People will listen to you that may not listen to me. Remember the open door earlier in example 5? People may open the door to you but wouldn't necessarily open it to me or vice versa. There are many reasons for that, but it's the truth. Like it or not people are guarded. This is why Jesus needs every one of us taking up the Mission of Love and sharing the light and the truth of Christ as the doors of opportunity open up.

Example Eight

*"For we are members of His body, of His flesh and of His bones. "For this reason, a man shall leave his father and mother and be joined to his wife, and the two shall become one flesh." **This is a great mystery,** but I speak concerning Christ and the church."*

Ephesians 5:30–32

This is a very important passage of scripture for Family Mission. Let's take a little extra time with this one. According to this scripture, marriage has a mandate upon it to be a witness to the relationship between Christ and the Church. The covenant love and one flesh dynamic in marriage is to give the world an example of becoming a Christian. It should show the world the power and pleasure of covenant love. No wonder the enemy targets marriage! Marriage is the foundation of the home and the family. Targeting marriage is strategic from the enemy's standpoint. Sadly, there are many marriages struggling. Even good marriages have battles that they've not overcome. Because of raw commitment and faithfulness, they have just accepted that's the way it is going to be. Many in ministry are struggling in their marriages too. In fact, even Kim and I know what it's like to struggle in marriage! That's right, we've had plenty of issues too. Holy Spirit used the truth of the Word of God to solve our struggles and heal our hearts.

When Kim and I discovered the Mission of Love it revolutionized our marriage and our home! We experienced a Divine Reset and so can you! **The truth of who we are IN CHRIST repositioned us and gave us a new perspective**, a new way to look at each other and ourselves. It gave our lives and marriage new meaning and purpose! We no longer just needed and pulled on each other. We understood what it meant to love each other.

The gospel of Jesus Christ actually heals the broken hearted, and once we are healed our heart no longer breaks! In other words, when you see how God sees people, you no longer get hurt BY people, you will only hurt FOR people. You will long for them to see and receive what healed your heart forever! Look at the Samaritan woman at the well in John 4. After one short conversation with Jesus (Love in the flesh) she ran to all the ones she used to hide from because of guilt, shame, and condemnation. Love had healed her heart. She was no longer vulnerable. She was free. She then invited all of them, "Come see a Man …"

As a Christian you should never let what people don't see change what they do see. If they just knew the truth of who they are, they would be different. Knowing that makes your heart hurt FOR them, not BECAUSE of them. It fuels prayer and intercession for them from the right place and with the right motive. You and I must not pray for people just from a place of how our lives are affected, but from a place of knowing their God given value, identity, and purpose. This is why Jesus could say, "Father, forgive them, they don't know what they are doing," (Luke 23:34). What does He mean, "they don't know what they are doing?" It's like Jesus was saying, "They don't see what I see. They don't know about their life what I know about their life." The gospel of Jesus Christ opens my eyes to see what He sees and to think like He thinks. Paul says we are to let this mind be in us which was in Christ Jesus (Philippians 2:5-11).

There is healing and wholeness available for all relationships. Imagine how relationships would heal and be restored if people were no longer hurt by one another. Please pause and let that sink in. Imagine how life would change if you could no longer be hurt by one another! The only hurt would be FOR others and not BY them. I know these truths will stretch you. They stretch me. Please don't be upset at what God is calling you to do. Don't let the devil trick you into thinking that this calling is stealing something from you.

Here's what Peter said about it in his first epistle. "For to this you were called because Christ also suffered for us, leaving us an example, that we should follow His steps: Who committed no sin, nor was deceit found in His mouth; who, when He was reviled, did not revile in return; when He suffered, He did not threaten, but committed Himself to Him who judges righteously…" Handling mistreatment like Christ is our calling! It's a major part of the Mission of Love!

The only thing that's being taken from you is a perspective that you were never intended to have from the beginning. It is possible to live the rest of your life and never be hurt by anyone ever again. I didn't say no one would ever mistreat you or mishandle you. I am saying that what He did for you matters more than what others can do to you. The only way this really works is if your life is no longer about you, but Christ in you and the hope of Him being seen and known through you. Your flesh may feel the sting or devastation of people's actions, but the power of Christ and truth and love quickly overwhelm that sting or devastation. The old phrase really is true, hurt people hurt people.

Living in the love of God is not accomplished by everyone treating you right or appreciating you. It's accomplished by His divine nature in you and how you see everyone in life. You've had your hurts healed by Christ and you want others to have their hurts healed by Christ. Knowing this is understanding the "why" behind the life God has given us. It's accomplished by seeing the Truth and walking in it. It's accomplished by understanding the Mission of Love. It's accomplished by taking up the cross and following Him.

Imagine how relationships would heal and be restored when you no longer need each other, but you live to love each other. If you need anything from any of the relationships in your life, then you're only going to be doing as well as how they see you or how they treat you. That's **not** solid ground! That's very unstable ground. It leaves you vulnerable and causes you to be up and down, in and out, for the rest of your life, all because of what you needed from someone. A need that can only be fulfilled by Christ Himself. This is why Jesus said to the woman at the well in John 4, "If you drink the water I offer you, you will never thirst again!"

If you let your perspective and reason for being change through the Gospel, then you live on the solid ground of being loved, no longer living on the unstable ground of needing to be loved! **Jesus Christ has the ability to satisfy your need of love completely and eternally.** I want to again point your attention to what Jesus said in John 4 while talking to the woman at the well of Samaria. "If you drink the water that I shall give you, you will NEVER THIRST AGAIN!" Because of the cross of Jesus Christ, being loved should never come into question again in your life! (See Romans 8:31-39) Nothing or no one can ever again separate you from love now that Jesus has come and healed and filled your heart! Glory to God!

It's commonly accepted that the people closest to you can hurt you the most. The people who say they love you end up hurting you. Why is that if they truly love you? It's because they really haven't understood love and the Mission of Love. It's because when most people say they love someone, they really mean they need or want them. What they're really saying is they like how that person makes them feel. The reason things often break down is because people place expectations, based on their needs, upon the people closest to them. This kind of relationship is destined to break down because of the pressure being placed on it. Relationships were never designed to carry that kind of pressure. This is why so many are hurting. This is why so many are broken. This is why the Mission of Love needs to be understood and embraced. We need a revival of the Mission of Love like never before!

Unless you start where He finished you will not run well, and relationships will break down all around you. Unless you're willing to let go of your story and embrace His story, relationships will break down. Unless you stop letting things matter more which do not matter most, relationships will continue to break down.

The gospel has many times just been a message that benefitted us and took us to heaven one day, but it did not transform us into love! We keep getting disappointed because of not receiving the benefits of the relationships. Instead, we should realize the privilege of Christ in us the hope of glory for this relationship. When we realize Christ is in us then we no longer have to put pressure on people. **We're fulfilled in Him and not by how people treat us.** We're fulfilled in Him and not by how circumstances are around us! That's a solid place to live. That's a steadfast and immovable place to live. Living in the place He has for you **makes you undevourable!** (I Peter 5:8-11)

This divine perspective allows you to see that your only responsibility in any relationship is to love; not to be loved! The Bible says in the book of Romans, "Owe no one anything but to love them." This revelation is certainly not limited to marriages. It works with someone you met for the very first time or someone you consider a close friend. Here at Family Mission headquarters, we like to say it this way: As born-again children of God we actually have His personality type; Christ is type A … Type Agape!

The truth and the Mission of Love is intended for every relationship dynamic. This is the passion burning in this book. If marriage is going to be the witness mandated by scripture, then you and I need to take up the cross at home and fulfill the Mission of Love. Marriage should be a witness to Him and His covenant love. Marriage should be a witness to the family of God and our union with Christ! Again, it's no wonder the enemy has attacked family and marriage so rigorously. No wonder he wants to confuse what family and marriage even looks like. Jesus came to revive the family mission.

Genesis teaches that creation was set in motion because God wanted a family! The enemy cannot afford for you to discover this. But it's TOO LATE! You already have and you're not backing down. This is the fire and passion burning throughout this book. I want to put the unquenchable fire of God in your heart! My goal is to help establish the Mission of Love in you. A mission that cannot fail because Love never fails!

Example Nine

*"Praying always with all prayer and supplication in the Spirit, being watchful to this end with all perseverance and supplication for all the saints—and for me, that utterance may be given to me, that I may open my mouth boldly to make known **the mystery of the Gospel**, for which I am an ambassador in chains; that in it I may speak boldly, as I ought to speak."*

Ephesians 6:18–20

Not everyone is going to be excited about your understanding of the mysteries of God. They persecuted Jesus. They persecuted the Apostle Paul. They persecuted the early Church. They have persecuted the Church all throughout history. They will persecute you too.

People who are content with a form of godliness will be challenged and exposed by people who walk in the power and glory of godliness, which is Christlikeness. Men and women whose ministries are based on a form of godliness will also be challenged and exposed by those who will not settle for anything less than the power and glory of godliness / Christlikeness.

I will teach about this more in the next chapter, but this was the original plan. Man was made in the image of God. Man was made in His image and likeness! (Genesis 1:26&27) That's not blasphemy, that's the Word of God. People have persecuted Christians for years saying, "You're just trying to act like Jesus!" Yes, that's right and we make no apologies for it. He told us to take up our cross and follow Him. By taking up the Mission of Love you need to know that persecution is just part of the life you're now called to live. Do you hear Him calling you? Do you hear Him inviting you to get out of the boat? Inviting you to get out on the water with Him as well? (Matthew 14:28)

Example Ten

*"Likewise, deacons must be reverent, not double-tongued, not given to much wine, not greedy for money, holding **the mystery of the faith** with a pure conscience."*

1 Timothy 3:8–9

You must endeavor to keep a pure motive in life, family, and ministry. You must maintain a pure conscience as you hold on to this mystery of the faith. Life can make you jaded. People can try to puff you up and people will try to tear you down. It's not always intentional, but there are definite hazards in this life. Jesus said, "In this life you will have tribulation, but be of good cheer I have overcome and **showed you therefore how to overcome,"** (John 16:33). Jesus never allowed sin against Him to produce, justify, or excuse sin in Him. Neither should you allow it. By the grace of God, He has given you a pure conscience through the new birth. He's also given you the Holy Spirit! Make sure to nurture and grow what He's given to you.

Paul mentions another huge issue where motive is concerned: greed! Greed for money is also greed for power. You and I have to be open to the Holy Spirit to convict us regarding our motives and attitudes. He will help you maintain a pure heart and a pure motive in the midst of a crooked and perverse generation. Your innocence and purity will be one of the reasons that you will stand out and shine. Let your integrity, purity of motive and conscience be a witness! A witness to the goodness, patience, and long-suffering of God.

Example Eleven

*"For I do not desire, brethren, that you should be ignorant of **this mystery,** lest you should be wise in your own opinion, that blindness in part has happened to Israel until the fullness of the Gentiles has come in."*

Romans 11:25

Romans 11 is an important chapter to look at. It reveals God's plan and the progression of redemption through the Old Testament into the New Testament. This chapter reveals both the goodness and severity of God. Please take time to read it in its entirety now. As Gentiles we should be thankful for the nation of Israel and realize God wants to call them to Christ. This is an essential facet of the mystery Paul is seeking to explain. I use the word facet because the mystery is just like a diamond. The more you turn it and look at it the more it sparkles. In this chapter I am not attempting to fully explain the mystery. I'm just trying to show you some of the sparkles. Your attitude towards Israel reveals how much or little you understand about the mystery of which Paul speaks.

Example Twelve

*"Now to Him who is able to establish you according to my Gospel and the preaching of Jesus Christ, according to the revelation of **the mystery** kept secret since the world began but now made manifest, and by the prophetic Scriptures made known to all nations, according to the commandment of the everlasting God, for obedience to the faith—to God, alone wise, be glory through Jesus Christ forever. Amen."*

Romans 16:25–27

What is Truth?

Discovering and walking out the mystery concerning your life comes through revelation. Helping someone else discover the mystery will also come by revelation. Be totally dependent upon the Holy Spirit, the Spirit of Truth, to discover and walk in truth. Communication is **not a simple transfer of information.** Information can be shared and even stolen, but revelation will never be stolen. **Revelation is reserved for those in personal relationship and for those who have ears to hear!**

That's what Jesus said in John 16:12. He said, *"I have many things to say to you now, but you can't hear them but when He (referring to Holy Spirit) comes, He will lead you and guide you into all the truth."* To solve the mystery, so to speak, requires the personal guidance of the Holy Spirit and those He anoints and sends into your life. I believe the anointing of God is upon this book. There is an impartation of the Holy Spirit available to you as you read. Divine grace deposits and truth impartations are my prayer for you!

Now let's look at examples of the mystery from the lips of Jesus from the Parable of the Sower:

> *"He answered and said to them, "Because it has been given to you to know **the mysteries of the kingdom of heaven**, but to them it has not been given."*

Matthew 13:11

*"And He said to them, "To you it has been giv-en to know **the mystery of the kingdom of God**; but to those who are outside, all things come in parables."*

Mark 4:11

*"And He said, "To you it has been given to know **the mysteries of the kingdom of God**, but to the rest it is given in parables, that, 'See-ing they may not see, and hearing they may not understand.'*

Luke 8:10

Jesus taught that parables were used to both reveal and hide the truth. The parables or illustrations He used hid the truth from some and revealed the truth to others! Wow! But here is the million-dollar question. How do you know if you have ears to hear? VERY SIMPLE. Do you want to act on what you discover? Do you want to become what you see in Him? Are you willing to take up your cross, the Mission of Love, and follow Him?

What is Truth?

Luke's account of the Parable of the Sower gives another critical ingredient. Jesus talked about those who received the word in a good and **honest heart** bringing forth fruit some 30, some 60, some 100-fold (Luke 8:15). An honest person loves truth and truthfulness. No wonder it's a key ingredient in hearing and receiving the truth. You're definitely called to both understand and reveal the mystery.

For many people life is a mystery. Even those people who think they have everything all figured out, like Saul of Tarsus, need to see the mystery of the gospel revealed! They need to see Jesus. Think about how many people tragically take their life after accomplishing magnificent success in the world's eyes! Stephen powerfully demonstrated and revealed the mystery to the Apostle Paul in Acts 7:59&60, *"And they (with Saul/Paul present and consenting) stoned Stephen as he was calling on God and saying, 'Lord Jesus, receive my spirit.' Then he knelt down and cried out with a loud voice, 'Lord, do not charge them with this sin.' And when he had said this, he fell asleep."*

When you understand the mystery of the Gospel, you will understand your God given value, identity, and purpose! When you understand the mystery of the Gospel, you will embrace the family mission, which is the Mission of Love. The family of God is an amazing family with an awesome mission! When you really understand the

Gospel, then you will understand the mystery behind life. You will understand the reason you're here on the Earth. You will understand the "why" behind your life/reason for being! You will discover that **there really are no more bad days: only opportunities to shine!**

Trusting God and shining now becomes the reason for living and it has the power to turn all your work into worship! That's right! All your life work becomes an expression of worship to God because you're trusting and being obedient in the work He gives you. Please do not limit this to spiritual work. Every segment of society needs someone shining. Every mountain of influence in culture today needs missionaries or ambassadors of Christ bringing the power and love of Christ to them. Every segment of society needs someone to reveal Christ right there - someone who understands the mystery of the Gospel and is able to reveal it!

CHAPTER TWO

A Divine Reset

The enemy has certainly been successful at twisting things and getting things out of place and out of course in the earth. Humanity has been heading in a self-centered and selfish direction for thousands of years now. Deception, pain, and dysfunction have compounded exponentially! **Then Jesus came on the scene and gave a clear witness of what it looks like for man to remain or abide in the love of the Father (John 15:10). I like to say He pushed the Divine Reset button.** The first Adam did not remain or abide in the love of the Father. The last Adam (Jesus) did remain and abide in the love of the Father.

In John 15 He then gave instructions to His disciples to remain in His love like He remained in the Father's love. He said there is no greater love than this, that a man lay his life down for his friends. He then called them friends! Please note, *friend* is actually a word reserved for "covenant partners" and not just "buddies!" When you understand this, then many of the things Jesus said finally make sense. For instance, when He told us to take up our cross and follow Him. What does that mean? It means you and I need to take up the Mission of Love and walk this agape life out every day, trusting like He trusted in the Mission of Love, living life everyday like He did - submitted to Love, no matter how hard life gets, always trusting the way of Love. **The Divine Reset is a glorious resetting of the Mission of Love in the heart of man. It's a glorious resetting of divine trust back in the heart of man.**

The Bible says Jesus was a man in whom was no guile or deceit (I Peter 2:22). His motive was never twisted, and His focus was only on your good! Love was His motive even when He offered a strong rebuke or other words that may have been hard to understand. In fact, one of His most powerful messages was also His most controversial message. It's found in John chapter 6. In His teaching, He talked about His followers eating His flesh and drinking His blood. What? That's right, He said, *"My flesh is meat indeed and my blood is drink indeed. He who eats My flesh and drinks My blood abides in Me, and I in him,"* (John 6,55,56). He was trying to get His followers to realize the goal of this thing was **to be one with Him:** to be like Him.

He wanted what was in Him to be in His followers. He was preparing a place **for** you and a place **in** you! Jesus was always teaching His disciples to do what He did and teach what He taught. A perfect example is when they were stranded in a storm and fearing for their lives in Matthew 14. Peter stepped up and solved the dilemma of whether or not they were seeing a ghost or if it was really Jesus walking on the water. Peter knew exactly what to do. He cried out to Jesus knowing that if it really was Him, then He would ask him to join Him on the water. Jesus didn't even hesitate, He said, "*Come.*" Notice the logic of Peter's request. Where did he get this logic? Why would he even think this way or come to this conclusion? Earlier the same day it was recorded in the account of Matthew 14:16. Before Jesus fed the 5000, He said, "*You give them something to eat.*" Why else would Jesus say in John 14:12 that the works that I do shall you do also, unless **His life was to be an example for you! Unless He truly was preparing a place for you? Unless He truly was establishing a Divine Reset for mankind.**

Yes, His life is a substitute. Yes, He is the Lamb of God. However, you can't forget that the Lamb of God took away the sins of the world. If your sins have been removed, then what are you left with? A Divine Reset of your innocence! Look at this verse in Colossians 1:20 in the Passion Translation, "*And by the blood of his cross, everything in heaven and earth is brought back to himself—back to its original intent, restored to innocence again!"*

Since this is true, you must learn to see Jesus not only as your Redeemer and Deliverer but also as your Example. His substitutional sacrifice removed your sin so you can now see what you're called to be like. Christlikeness really is the goal and your destiny (Romans 8:29). Everything He did was so you can move into **the place** He prepared for you! It's why He can now say, "Follow Me." It's why He can tell a man named Peter, "Come, join Me on the water." It's why He can tell His disciples, "You give them something to eat." It's why He can tell His disciples, "All power in Heaven and Earth is given unto Me, Go ye therefore ..."

No matter what your past or current circumstances are, you are called to experience a Divine Reset. Furthermore, you are privileged and called to help others get their lives reset by the power of God. Reset to the original purpose for man. Reset to innocence with our Father in Heaven. **Everyone needs to learn how to live in the place Jesus prepared for them!**

The reality is some people will never be touched by Jesus no matter how relevant or cool we make our church services. They will only be touched when someone like you, filled with love, touches their life! Someone like you fulfilling the Mission of Love! Someone like you who has been born-again. Divinely Reset. You are called to be under the Mission of Love. That's what Jesus made very clear in His life and teaching. He then said to follow Him. Let's now take a look at what a couple of dictionaries give us regarding a definition of a reset.

Definition of RESET

(Merriam Websters) To move (something) back to an original place or position. Ex. To put a broken bone back in the correct position for healing. Ex. To put (a gem) into a new piece or setting.

(Oxford) To Set Again or Differently Synonyms for Reset are (Restart, Reboot, Recalibrate) Ex. On a computer the reset button clears the memory and causes it to reboot!

Jesus came so that we could be born-again. Using Webster's definition Jesus came so that we could Restart, Reboot, and Recalibrate.

In Hebrews 9 we are now going to see that Jesus came to **set things straight!**

"Seeing that that first [outer portion of the] tabernacle was a parable (a visible symbol or type or picture of the present age). In it gifts and

*sacrifices are offered, and yet are incapable of perfecting the conscience or of cleansing and renewing the inner man of the worshiper. For [the ceremonies] deal only with clean and unclean meats and drinks and different washings, [mere] external rules and regulations for the body imposed to tide the worshipers over **until the time of setting things straight [of reformation, of the complete new order when Christ, the Messiah, shall establish the reality of what these things foreshadow—a better covenant].***"

Hebrews 9:9-10 AMPC

Jesus came to set things straight.

Jesus came for a time of reformation.

Jesus came to set up the complete new order.

Jesus established a better covenant.

Hebrews 9:12-14 goes on to say, "Not with the blood of goats and calves, but with His own blood He entered the Most Holy Place once for all, having obtained eternal redemption. For if the blood of bulls and goats and the ashes of a heifer, sprinkling the unclean, sanctifies for the purifying of the flesh, **how much more shall the blood of Christ, who through the eternal Spirit offered Himself**

without spot to God, cleanse your conscience from dead works to serve the living God?"

> *Then right on into the next chapter it says, "For the law, having a shadow of the good things to come, and not the very image of the things, can never with these same sacrifices, which they offer continually year by year, make those who approach perfect. For then would they not have ceased to be offered? For the* **worshipers, once purified, would have had no more consciousness of sins.** *But in those sacrifices, there is a reminder of sins every year. For it is not possible that the blood of bulls and goats could take away sins."*

Hebrews 10:1-4

Paul says it like this in Colossians 1:20 TPT, "*And by the blood of his cross, everything in heaven and earth is brought back to himself—back to its original intent, restored to innocence again!*"

With all this in mind … repenting is simply returning to the top! Repenting is going back where you belong. You are seated with Jesus in Heavenly Places; the place He prepared for you.

In order to better understand a Divine Reset and coming back to the top where you belong, let's take a closer look at original intent and your divine origin. Here's a tremendous passage found in the Passion Translation.

"If you listen to the Word and don't live out the message you hear, you become like the person who looks in the mirror of the Word to discover the reflection of his face in the beginning. You perceive how God sees you in the mirror of the Word, but then you go out and forget **your divine origin.** *"*

James (Jacob) 1:23-24 TPT

Did you catch that? Your divine origin. Yes, your physical body was the result of your parents' biological make up. But your spirit came from God and is in the image and likeness of God according to Genesis, the book of beginnings. Here's what Genesis records about man's beginning and the beginning of the family of God.

"Then God said, **'Let Us make man in Our image, according to Our likeness;** *let them have dominion over the fish of the sea, over the birds of the air, and over the cattle, over all the earth and over every creeping ting that creeps on the earth.'* **So, God created man in His own**

image; in the image of God, He created him; male and female He created them. *And the Lord God formed man of the dust of the ground and breathed into his nostrils the breath of life; and man became a living being. Then the Lord God caused a deep sleep to fall on Adam, and he slept; and He took one of his ribs and closed up the flesh in its place. Then the rib which the Lord God had taken from man He made into a woman, and He brought her to the man. And Adam said, 'This is now bone of my bones and flesh of my flesh; She shall be called Woman, because she was taken out of Man.' Therefore, a man shall leave his father and mother and be joined to his wife, and they shall become one flesh. And they were both naked, the man and his wife, and were not ashamed."*

Genesis 1:26,27, 2:7,21-25

Before we go too far studying a fallen man, we need to study man in the beginning. Man before he fell and was separated from God. We're not given any definitive clues as to how long Adam and Eve walked with God before the fall. When people refer to the fall of man, they are referring to what happened when man sinned. God said in the day you sin, separate from love, you will die!

Man did die. He didn't drop dead physically. We often hear people say that he died spiritually. But what does that really mean?

He was separated from God. Who is God? God is Love (I John 4:8). God is Light (I John 1:6). Man was separated from love and the light went out. It actually took several hundred years for his physical body to die. However, man died and was separated instantly just like God said. He was separated from light. He was separated from love.

What does it mean to be separated from the light and love of God? One simple way I could explain it is His perspective shifted. The why behind his life shifted. His motive turned inward. He began to think like a survivor instead of a son. This is why we say man fell. Oh, how far we have fallen. Humanity is not evolving like some would like you to think. Humanity is trying to recover from an incredibly long fall. Humanity needs to be born-again. Humanity needs a divine reset! The more you begin to understand the mystery Paul reveals, the more you will begin to see how far man actually fell!

The life of Jesus actually shows you how far man fell. Jesus is called the last Adam for a reason. Yes, He is the Son of God, but He is also the son of Man. Not 50% God, 50% man. This isn't some sort of Greek mythology.

Jesus is 100% God, and 100% man. Let that sink in! That's original intent revealed. That's a revelation! **I Corinthians 15:49 says, *"as we have borne the image of the man of dust, we shall also bear the image of the Heavenly Man."***

It's not healthy as Christians to study the fallen man more than you study the Heavenly Man! Even in the arena of counterfeiting money, those who work to find counterfeits do not try to learn all the different kinds of counterfeits. **They study the real thing.** They study the **original**. When you completely understand the real or the original then the counterfeits will just stand out.

From the very beginning God was starting a family. The original intent was a family! Adam and Eve were husband and wife. God was not starting a religion; **He was beginning a family! A family that was then given a mission! A dominion mandate to replenish the earth.**

> *"Wives, submit to your own husbands, as to the Lord. For the husband is head of the wife, as also Christ is head of the church; and He is the Savior of the body. Therefore, just as the church is subject to Christ, so let the wives be to their own husbands in everything. Husbands, love your wives, just as Christ also loved the church and gave Himself for her, that He might*

*sanctify and cleanse her with the washing of water by the word, that He might present her to Himself **a glorious church,** not having spot or wrinkle or any such thing, but that she should be holy and without blemish. So, husbands ought to love their own wives as their own bodies; he who loves his wife loves himself. For no one ever hated his own flesh, but nourishes and cherishes it, just as the Lord does **the church**. For we are members of His body, of His flesh and of His bones. ‹For this reason a man shall leave his father and mother and be joined to his wife, and the two shall become one flesh.' **This is a great mystery, but I speak concerning Christ and the Church.** Nevertheless, let each one of you in particular so love his own wife as himself, and let the wife see that she respects her husband."*

Ephesians 5:22-33

It is scripturally unreasonable to think a glorious church will come forth without marriage and family coming forth into the full glory they had in the beginning. As I discussed in the last chapter this is a great mystery! A mystery that He fully expects for you to understand. **This also reveals the original mission of man!**

He gave His Son and the Holy Spirit so that you could fully understand this great mystery. He wants you to fully understand **your place**!

Jesus came to seek and save that which was lost. Sometimes we only think of Him coming to save **who** was lost. Yes, He will leave the 99 and come after the one. However, something was lost that Jesus was seeking and saving. He came to get the image and identity of mankind back! He came to get your purpose back. He came to show the real value and mission of man! **He came to get His family back**. He came to give humanity a good look at what it looks like when a man remains in **the place** of our Father's love (John 15:10)!

In the Garden of Eden, the enemy hijacked the image and vision of man, and ever since then he's been using man to build his counter kingdom. A kingdom built on self rather than love! Jesus came to get the image and vision back in man so God could once again build His family and Kingdom with man. A Kingdom of Love! He came to pursue you like a man pursues his wife. The gospel then becomes God's invitation to humanity to be one with Him, to be one with Him again like it was in the beginning! Back to **a place** of oneness. No wonder the family is under attack by the enemy. No wonder marriage is under the attack of the enemy. No wonder both family and marriage have become a source of such pain and confusion. **It's because marriage and family carry the original plan and purpose for man**. Covenant family is an eternal framework that God wants to build *with* and *upon*! Covenant family is going to be the expression of the glorious church. The glorious church is called to reveal the family of God and the Mission of Love. Your original value, identity and purpose is revealed in biblical marriage and family!

Do not be ashamed or condemned if your family and marriage look nothing like the biblical image. God has already rolled up His sleeves and proven His relentless love and His redemptive powers! God has clearly proven that's He's not afraid of any family problems. What He needs from you is to agree with Him concerning His plan and His purpose and then allow the Holy Spirit to begin His work.

You may be the first person in your family to be a Christian and have a personal relationship with God through Christ. Thank God you are positioned in **a place** to give your family a new future. *Don't take that as pressure, rather embrace it as a privilege.* **God chose you!** Jesus taught this principle in John 15:16. He said, "You did not choose me, but I chose you." He said in another place, "No man comes to the Father except the Father draws them" (John 6:44).

He's drawing you. He wants you close to Him. He wants you to know Him intimately! **Your life with Christ in God becomes a seed of redemption in your home and family.**

The enemy cannot afford for you to understand who you are from the beginning. He cannot afford for you to understand that Jesus came to remove your sin so He could show you who you were from the beginning. He cannot afford for you to be born-again and understand all that really means. He cannot afford for you to have an intimate relationship with Holy Spirit and to be baptized in the Spirit with Holy Fire! He cannot afford for Christ to really live in you and live through you like Paul said in Galatians 2:20. Somebody shout it out, **"Too late!"** Let's make him regret that he ever touched our lives with his filthy selfish lies! The original mission or purpose was a family. The original mission or purpose was the Mission of Love.

Another important thing that happens in a Divine Reset is the holy fear of the Lord is reset in your life. The fear of the Lord is perfect trust in the Father and His Word. Let me ask you a question. What was really lost in the Garden of Eden? The root of all that was lost is **a Father lost the TRUST of His son and daughter!** His goodness and character were brought into question by the accuser, Satan. What was it that Jesus reset and restored for man? He reset and restored a place of perfect trust with the Father.

What was lost in the Garden of Eden was restored in the Garden of Gethsemane. When Jesus sweat great drops of blood submitting and trusting the Father, **TRUST** was being restored. There was a Divine Reset of trust between God and man. This kind of perfect trust and this kind of perfect love is one of the most important facets of what the Bible calls the fear of the Lord. Jesus restored the honor the Heavenly Father deserves in the life of a man!

How do we know that Adam and Eve lost their trust? Because when Love & Light & Truth came in, they were covering, hiding, blaming, and making excuses. Does that sound familiar?

*"Then the eyes of both of them were opened, and they knew that they were naked; and **they sewed fig leaves together and made themselves coverings.** And they heard the sound of the Lord God walking in the garden in the cool of the day, and Adam and his wife **hid themselves** from the presence of the Lord God among the trees of the garden. Then the Lord God called to Adam and said to him, ‹Where are you?' So, he said,'"I heard Your voice in the garden, and I was afraid because I was naked; and **I hid myself.'** And He said,'"who told you that you were*

naked? Have you eaten from the tree of which I commanded you that you should not eat?' **Then the man said, ‹The woman whom You gave to be with me, she gave me of the tree, and I ate.'** *And the Lord God said to the woman,' "What is this you have done?'* **The woman said, 'The serpent deceived me, and I ate.'"**

Genesis 3:7-13

When Light and Love come you must resist the urge to cover, hide, blame, and make excuses. You must trust in the goodness of God. His goodness to confront you and His goodness to transform you by His love.

It's important that you honor all the facets of Love's character. Yes, He is merciful, and His throne is a throne of Grace. He is also just, and He is Holy! <u>These are not competing realities, but harmonious ones</u>. I heard one person say the fear of the Lord is beauty that makes you tremble! Isn't that powerful? God will not pervert His justice or integrity for anyone. When He forgives you, it's because He has made righteous and legal provisions for it. Yes, you relate to Him as Abba Father and covenant Friend. But you also relate to Him as the righteous Judge over all of creation.

Through His justice He has intentionally provided a way for His merciful nature to be seen and known. The

Bible is clear; Love will both correct and warn. Hebrews 12:5-11 says that if we are without correction, then we're not legitimate children. A real, loving warning is not intended to scare or even threaten. In fact, **all real communication ceases in a threatening environment**. God gave both instructions and warnings to Adam in the Garden of Eden. This was in a perfect environment. You could say it was a totally and fully graced environment. Yet Love gave both boundaries and warnings. Love enforced and stood behind those boundaries and warnings!

I recommend all believers read the first three chapters of Revelation often. It's healthy to keep Jesus before your eyes as a glorified Lord and King. Perhaps you could take a few minutes right now, put this book down, and read those three chapters. When you do, you will notice how Jesus looks now and how He talks to the Church. You will notice the fire in His eyes! He is absolute Grace, Truth, Love, Mercy, and Justice. **None of these realities are in competition.**

Some people have gotten the idea that the God of the Old Testament and the God of the New Testament are somehow two different Gods. Nothing could be further from the truth. Yes, there's two different covenants, but He's One God! It helps to understand that the Bible is progressive revelation of the same God! In fact, His purpose and mission has not changed. We changed, but thank God, He didn't give up on us. Thank God He never lost sight of who we were even when we were buried in our sin and rebellion. **Thank God He was willing to dig with the shovel of the cross and remove our sin so our eternal value, identity and purpose could be revealed!**

Here's another way to explain it. Maybe your family has lived in a number of different houses throughout the years, but you're the same family. You were under a number of different roofs, but again you're the same family. God has related to humanity in and through a number of different covenants, but He has not changed. He's the same yesterday, today and forever. He said, *"I am the Lord and I change not," (Malachi 3:6).*

Here's maybe a funny way to look at it. Some people think God in the Old Covenant is like your parents and God in the New Covenant is like your grandparents. Some have mistakenly thought that God has loosened the standards in the New Testament and He's not near as strict. Nothing could be further from the truth. Jesus said these words multiple times in Matthew 5, "You've heard it said … but I say unto you." No longer can I simply not murder; I can't let my heart be angry and judgmental towards others.

Sounds like grace has raised the standard, not lowered it.

In addition to Revelation chapters 1-3, the short epistle of Jude is another great read. Jude addresses the issues we're dealing with in our day. Some are turning the grace of our Lord Jesus Christ into lewdness and lack of restraint. They have lost the fear of God! Jude closes his short letter talking about the importance of praying in the Holy Ghost **and keeping yourself in the love of God and looking for the mercy of our Lord Jesus Christ unto eternal life.** That's abiding in <u>the place He prepared for you</u>. He says, "And on some have compassion, making a distinction; but others save with fear, pulling them out of the fire, hating even the garment defiled by the flesh" (Jude 20-22).

Yes, it is the goodness of God that leads men to repentance, but how can you fully grasp the goodness of God until you consider the consequences of His perfect justice and holiness upon your sin and sinfulness. The movie *The Passion* was a great way to feel the price of our sin. Yet as graphic as it was it still could not fully depict the price He paid and the suffering He experienced spirit, soul, and body. It's incredibly important to understand that God's **goodness has never violated His justice and integrity!** The Bible calls Him the righteous Judge of all the earth (II Timothy 4:8). He says that vengeance belongs to Him

(Romans 12:19)! It doesn't belong to us; it belongs to Him! The forgiveness of God offered in the Gospel is just as much an act of justice and it is mercy. Please let that sink in and take root in your heart.

You could even look at the two beams forming the cross just that way. The cross is where justice and mercy came together. In other words, Jesus is on the cross because His Father is both just and merciful. The cross perfectly expresses His righteousness and His compassion. Praise God, He made mercy prevail right in the midst of His justice. **Love never fails! There is no Divine Reset and no new birth without the cross of Jesus Christ.**

As you grow in love, you're growing in God. You cannot just leave out portions of His character to focus on what you want from Him. You cannot afford a Gospel that just benefits you and does not transform you into His image. This is why you find on all of our social media Family Mission materials #TruthThatTransforms and #DivineReset. We must be seeking to be like Him. He is holy and He is pure!

Romans 8:38-39 says that nothing can separate us from the love of God. His love for us should be settled forever and NEVER ever come into question again. You should NEVER again live a day in need of love. You should NEVER again put that pressure on anyone again.

All relationships will eventually break down and fall apart under that kind of pressure. At a minimum, the relationship will just limp along. Please quit putting pressure on people in your life once you're born-again, once you've experienced a Divine Reset and been filled with His love (Romans 5:5).

Once you're born-again you have the privilege of seeing people as God sees them. You have the privilege of seeing them from Love's perspective. No longer the perspective of needing love from them. For you have taken a drink of Living Water from the Well of Salvation: Jesus. Now you no longer have to thirst for their love. You have been satisfied and been filled by His perfect Love! That need was completely met by God your Father, His Son, and the precious Holy Spirit!

Here's a few more thoughts connecting the Divine Reset with the fear of the Lord being restored in your life. In Isaiah 11, the prophet is referring to Jesus as the Root of Jesse. Jesse was King David's father and Jesus is called the Son of David in His lineage as the Messiah. In Isaiah 11:1-5 there are many references to the Fear of the Lord in His life! In this passage it refers to the Spirit of God resting upon Him and describes several expressions of the Spirit of God. It says **the Spirit of the fear of the Lord** will rest upon Him and His delight is in **the fear of the Lord!** It says He will be made of quick understanding in **the fear of the Lord.** That is so important to realize.

Having revelation and understanding in the fear of the Lord will actually deepen Christlikeness and your maturity in love. _It will also actually increase the joy we walk in!_ For the Bible says, He was anointed with the oil (anointing) of joy above all His companions. Once again, these attributes of God are not competing realities but completing realities. Scripture records in Isaiah 6 that in God's presence mighty angels cry out continually HOLY, HOLY, HOLY. Yet in Psalms 16:11 King David the worshipper says that in the presence of the Lord is the FULLNESS OF JOY! **In His Holy presence we see the fullness of joy and pleasures for evermore! Holy and happy are in the same space.**

Here is a testimony that will perhaps help along these lines. I remember how the Lord taught me this early in my walk with Him. I was endeavoring to read through the Bible in a year for the first time. I kept getting hung up in Exodus, Leviticus, and Deuteronomy. I had the thought, "Wow God, you sure are picky about things." No, the lightning didn't strike. I went on to say as sincerely and humbly as I could, "What does all this mean?" I did learn

years later many of the countless amazing types and shadows contained in the details of the Old Testament. Everything points to Jesus! But what I heard God speak to me
that day was worth more to me than any type or shadow
I have studied out over the years. In fact, it was the first
time in my life of faith that I had a personal question, and
I knew He answered me.

The God of all creation answered a question for Mark
Spellman in the little town of Trenton, Missouri! Would
you like to hear what He told me when I asked Him, "What
do all these details mean?" He said, "Mark, these passages
reveal **The Privilege of My Presence!"**

The Privilege of My Presence

I might add today, the privilege of **the place I have
prepared for you.** Those words marked me for life! Everything I learned about those types and shadows pointing
to who Christ is and why He came helped me. However,
nothing helps me more in life than hearing Him personally
for myself! I actually had the Author of the Bible give me
some personal commentary. **The Bible is the only book
where the Author is actually in love with the reader!**

I've also heard it said that we do not just read the Bible, but the Bible actually reads us!

Here's some good news, this kind of relationship is available to every single one of His children. Thank God the Bible is not just about getting you to Heaven. It's more about getting Who's in Heaven inside of you! Glory to God! **You must never forget what a joy, privilege, and honor it is to be indwelled by Love Himself.**

I have another testimony that I would like to share with you regarding the fear of the Lord and the purpose for the Divine Reset. This experience happened early one morning. Right as I was coming awake, I had a little vision. I saw the throne of God and a Lamb came walking right out of the midst of it. I knew exactly in my mind that this vision came right out of the Revelation.

> *"So I wept much, because no one was found worthy to open and read the scroll, or to look at it. But one of the elders said to me, ‹**Do not weep. Behold, the Lion of the tribe of Judah, the Root of David, has prevailed to open the scroll and to loose its seven seals.'** And I looked, and behold, in the midst of the throne and of the four living creatures, and in the*

*midst of the elders, stood **a Lamb as though it
had been slain,** having seven horns and seven
eyes, which are the seven Spirits of God sent
out into all the earth. Then He came and took
the scroll out of the right hand of Him who sat
on the throne."*

Revelation 5:4-7

Right then, the Holy Spirit whispered to me, **"Only a
Lamb is worthy of sovereignty!"** This has marked my
life eternally. Once again these are not competing realities
but completing ones. Only a Lamb is worthy of sovereign
authority and power! What could be more intimidating
than standing in front of someone with absolute omnipo-
tent power and authority? Yet the Lion and the Lamb are
the same in the throne of God.

**Only a lamb will be given the ability to roar like a
lion throughout eternity!** I would suggest to you that this
is a major and overarching lesson we learn from the book
of the Revelation. Of all the things you can learn from its
pages do not miss the throne of all justice and grace! Learn
to come boldly to this throne. Let the Holy Spirit teach
you how to rule and reign with Him! To this very day I am
pressing into understanding more and more of **the place**
He prepared for us.

Jesus was seen as a lamb through His perfect trust and love of the Father. Therefore, He will roar as a lion throughout the ages. When He comes in judgement the Bible says they will flee in terror from the wrath of the Lamb (Revelation 6:16). A Divine Reset of trust is so very important. Why? Because life and relationships are all about trust! Who or what is leading you? Where and in whom is your trust? These are all very important questions we need to regularly answer.

Faith is equal to trust when you use biblical definitions. Why? Because faith is relational not just informational. Faith is relational, not just theological. For instance, trusting people is much different than trusting in the chair that you are sitting in. It was a lack of faith or trust that kept the first generation of Israel out of their inheritance and the same thing can keep you out of yours! Look at this verse in Hebrews 4:1-3 AMPC:

> *"THEREFORE, WHILE the promise of entering His rest still holds and is offered [today],* ***let us be afraid [to distrust it]****, lest any of you should think he has come too late and has come short of [reaching] it. For indeed we have had the glad tidings [Gospel of God] proclaimed to us just as truly as they [the Israelites of old did*

when the good news of deliverance from bon
*came to them]; **but the message they heard***
did not benefit them, because it was not mixed
with faith (with the leaning of the entire per-
sonality on God in absolute trust and confi-
dence in His power, wisdom, and goodness)
*by those who heard it; **neither were they united***
in faith with the ones [Joshua and Caleb] who
heard (did believe). For we who have believed
(adhered to and trusted in and relied on God)
do enter that rest…"

Absolute TRUST AND CONFIDENCE in **His** power, wisdom & goodness! That is a powerful statement. That is a powerful truth! Declare this today over your life and relationship with the Lord: *"I have absolute trust and confidence in His power, wisdom, and goodness. Nothing can steal my trust and confidence in Him!"*

Trust is the core issue addressed in the Bible. Psalms 118:8 says, *"It is better to trust in the Lord Than to put confidence in man."* There are exactly 594 chapters before and after Psalm 118. That's a total of 1118! Psalm 117 is the shortest chapter in the Bible and Psalm 119 is the longest chapter in the Bible. So, there it is literally at the center or core of the Bible. Do you trust in the Lord, or do you put your confidence in man? This is why Jesus came for a Divine Reset- to take our trust out of man and put it back in God our Father.

Jesus said it this way in John 15:9-10, *"As the Father loved Me, I also have loved you;* **abide in My love.** <u>*If you keep My commandments, you will abide in My love,*</u> *just as* ***I have kept My Father's commandments and abide in His love."***

Trust is at the root of our worship as defined in Genesis 22. The very first place we see the word *worship* used in the Bible. The whole next chapter will deal further with this connection of trust and worship. Paul perfectly explains his faith in relational terms in II Timothy 1:12, *"For this reason I also suffer these things; nevertheless, I am not ashamed,* ***for I know whom I have believed*** *(trusted) and am persuaded that He is able to keep what I have committed to Him until that Day."*

Notice he didn't say WHAT he believed but **WHO he believed!** It's not about what you believe, but rather Who you are believing! I think we just found the secret of how Paul endured all that He endured without weakening or backing down.

A Divine Reset is not about pushing a "button" on some machine. It's about being born-again. It's about coming back to the top with God. Jesus came to take you back to the place man had with God in the beginning. Walking and living in this will require constant renewing of the mind to root out all the lies that life has told you about who God is and who you are. Let's continue our journey together as we now look further at your life of worship.

CHAPTER THREE

True Worshippers

Worship is sure a popular word today and like the word love it is often used causally and easily. It means various things depending on who's using it. In some cases, it's been reduced to the slow songs that follow the fast songs in our church services. Jesus has something very important to say about worship in John chapter 4:23,24. He said the hour now is when **true worshippers** would worship the Father in spirit and in truth. In fact, He said the Father is seeking such to worship Him. This obviously means so much more than singing to Him or singing about Him.

Singing is a powerful thing to do together. Remember Paul and Silas in Acts 16? They were imprisoned and in chains in a Philippian jail. At midnight they decided to sing some songs! That's right. No instruments, just voices. Paul and Silas were the instruments as they sang praises to God. I would say that was an expression of true worship and trust for sure. No doubt God heard them singing and received their worship because of what happened next. The Bible says they sang loud enough for the other prisoners to hear them. Then the prison began to shake, **all the prison doors were opened, and everyone's chains were loosed!**

It probably wasn't just the song choice that was the issue. In worship services today if something powerful is released as we sing a particular song, then you better believe we're going to be singing that song again when we need something to happen in a service. Songs that contain revelation and truth are a powerful way for us to connect together and focus on Him, but the song is not some unseen switch releasing blessings as we gather. It's the heart of trust released by true worshippers in the room.

In John 4:23,24 Jesus teaches us some powerful things regarding worship. First of all, He uses a clarifying word - *true* worshippers. What is that all about? Sounds like what Paul was saying when he described the faith of his spiritual son Timothy (II Timothy 1:5). He called Timothy's faith "unfeigned." That's a King James word for genuine or real. If Paul had to qualify Timothy's faith as real or genuine that lets us know that there must be a false or pretend faith. This is likely what Jesus is letting us know when He uses the descriptive term *true* worshippers, meaning there could be a false or even pretend worship.

Let me share a testimony from the first few years I was walking with the Lord. My heart was on fire for the Lord and there was no question of my zeal for Him and His church. When I was in services where we sang, I was all in, whether I was on key or not! I always figured that mine was the joyful noise the Bible spoke about. Anyway, I found myself alone one time worshipping the Lord using words that I had learned in church, words that I had heard other believers use.

One specific time the Holy Spirit just interrupted my worship and asked me, "What are you saying?" I said, "I'm saying, 'Hallelujah!'" He said, "What does that mean?" I said, "Actually, I don't know!" He then told me it would be better for me to use the word *WOW* or *AWESOME* or some other word I understood than to use borrowed phrases. He used the term *borrowed phrases*. I had never heard of that before, but I knew exactly what He was saying. I made the adjustment immediately. No more borrowed phrases for me! Why don't you make the same commitment today and say with me, "No more borrowed phrases!"

This was the exact same issue Jesus had to deal with in His ministry one day. There was a Syrophoenician woman who came to Him one day, desperate to get deliverance for her daughter (Matthew 15:21-28). She came to Him crying out "Oh Lord, Thou Son of David have mercy on me!" That's exactly what Blind Bartimaeus said when he got healed by Jesus. That's what many others said when they called upon Jesus for help.

Recognizing Him as the Messiah, the King of Israel, in the lineage of David was important. However, this Syrophoenician woman was not a woman of the covenants of Israel. She was not even a Jewish proselyte. She was using what Holy Spirit taught me that day as *borrowed phrases*. Just saying what we think we are supposed to say. Just using words to get something from God and bypassing real relational faith or trust. Remember we talked about that in the last chapter. It's not about what we believe, it's about **who we are believing or trusting.**

This Syrophoenician had quite a journey getting to a place of genuine, sincere relational faith. She had to press through the disciples telling her to leave them alone. She had to press through Jesus ignoring her initially. She had to press through Jesus saying, "It's not right to take the children's bread and cast it to dogs!" Wait a minute; what? Did Jesus call her a dog? Before you rush to conclusions about this, let me ask you a question. Is Jesus Love in the flesh? Of course, He is. **Anything Jesus says is always in and of love, and it's the truth.**

When this woman came to Jesus, she told Him her daughter was severely possessed of devils. You don't have a daughter severely possessed with devils unless there's some issues at home. Not to mention the Syrophoenician people did not have a really good reputation for their culture and conduct. This beautiful woman hung in there through it all and showed the persistence of true faith and true trusting worship!

Eventually she shifted from borrowed phrases to a genuine cry, saying, "TRUTH LORD, yet even the little dogs eat the crumbs which fall from the master's table!" Humility and persistence are important ingredients to true faith and true trusting worship. To that genuine and honest response, He said, "Oh woman, GREAT IS YOUR FAITH! Let it be to you as your desire." She is one of only two people about whom Jesus ever said their faith was great! The other was the Centurion in Matthew 8.

Great faith produces great worship!

When she returned home, she found her daughter totally set free! Praise God. If you are going to be a true worshipper, you're going to have to be humble, persistent, and completely genuine with the Lord. You are going to have to make your worship relational. You're going to have to let Jesus speak to you about any borrowed phrases or borrowed faith in your life.

Let's now look at another thing that the Jesus is teaching about worship. He said the Father is seeking true worshippers. Why is God seeking true worshippers? Is He seeking worship? Or is He seeking the worshiper? Without any doubt it's the worshipper! God doesn't NEED your worship. God WANTS to be with His worshipper. The Holy Spirit said it this way to my heart. He said the Father is seeking worshippers because **He's seeking intimacy, agreement, and partnership with us!** Worship is all about intimacy, agreement, and partnership. A song is a worship song if it fuels your intimacy, agreement, and partnership. A worship service is one that fuels your intimacy, agreement, and partnership with Him.

Intimacy

Agreement

Partnership

Look at how most of our traditional worship gatherings are planned out. First, we sing about the Lord and then other songs directly to the Lord. That's **intimacy**. Then we hear the word of God taught or preached. That's how you adjust your thinking and believing to get into **agreement** with Him. Always remember that you adjust to Him, not the other way around. Then you walk out the doors and shine as the light of the world. Shining at home and at work. That's **partnership**. This intimacy, agreement, and partnership has everything to do with you working with Him in the Mission of Love!

Isn't this also what marriage is all about? Remember we talked about the mandate scripture gives marriage in Ephesians 5 to be a witness of Christ and the Church. The covenant of marriage is about intimacy, agreement, and partnership on all levels. Isn't this what family is about? Family is also about intimacy, agreement, and partnership. This is why it's so important to understand what it means to be a true worshipper. Your marriage and family will go from glory to glory through true worship. Your individual life will go from glory to glory as you live a life of true worship.

Let's look at one more thing Jesus is teaching about God seeking true worshippers. The fact that He's seeking reveals He is the initiator! Who loved whom first? (I John 4:19) We love Him because He first loved us, right? Who actually chose whom first? Jesus said you didn't choose Me, but I have chosen you (John 15). It says in Ephesians chapter 1 that you were chosen before the foundations of the world! Now that will stretch your brain way out! But it's true. Who found whom first? Jesus said in Luke 15 that He came to seek and save that which was lost.

The Bible says He is the Author and Finisher of your faith! So, Him seeking is Him initiating. The song <u>I Have Decided to Follow Jesus</u> is often sung during altar calls. Let's examine that a bit. Yes, love requires a choice. Yes, you have to choose, but you can't make that choice unless the Father draws you to Himself by His Spirit. No, He will not force you, and no, He won't make you choose Him. But you could not choose Him if He were not choosing, convicting, convincing, and drawing you with His Spirit.

Here's another thought to consider. As I've stated the cross revealed your value to God. He didn't pay such a high price for something or someone that is not of great value. How valuable then are you to God? You are worth the life of His only begotten Son! This should forever settle and remove any self-worth issues that you might have. I heard a comedian once say, "When the Creator of all matter says that you matter, YOU MATTER!" That's kind of cheesy, but it makes the point. You are extremely valuable to God. You matter!

When you go to sell a house or a car, what do you do first? You get an appraisal. Why? So that people buying it know they are getting a good deal. At the end of the day, you want to be happy with what you get, and they want to be happy with what they paid. Right? Do you think God is happy with what He paid? Do you think He's happy with what He got?

Hebrews 12:2 says for the joy set before Him He endured the cross. You were the joy set before Him. He's happy to have you. You are worth it to Him.

On the road to Golgotha, Luke's Gospel account records Jesus as He told all those weeping for Him, "Don't weep for Me…" (Luke 23:28). One time I asked the Lord why He said, "Don't weep for Me." He spoke back to my spirit and said, "BECAUSE I'M GETTING EXACTLY WHAT I WANT!" Wow, that's a powerful revelation. He's getting exactly what He wanted. Did He want the beating? Did He want the scourging? Did He want the mocking? No … He wanted YOU. He was getting you by removing your sin and revealing your value.

If the cross is truly revealing your value, then you could say that God is providing His appraisal of you. An appraisal is simply the act or process of developing an opinion of value. The root of the word *appraisal* is obviously "praise." The cross of Jesus Christ clearly shows that God has an extremely high opinion regarding you and your value. The cross is a high appraisal for sure!

When you sing songs of praise to God, what are you doing? One thing you're doing is singing and declaring your opinion of His value to you. Jesus spoke in John 5:44 regarding how important it is to seek and know God's opinion of you. "How can you believe, who receive honor from one another, and do not seek the honor that comes from the only God." Honor from God only comes to those He values, approves of, and is pleased with.

What do you do when you are pleased with your children or grandchildren and want to express it to them? You offer them honor or praise in some form or fashion. You will likely brag on them to all your friends or even go on social media with pictures and comments! Well, God is a parent too. He may not have Facebook, but He has a Book, and He has a Face. The high priestly blessing of Aaron says this:

The Lord bless you and keep you.

The Lord make His face to shine upon you.

The Lord lift up His countenance upon you.

The Lord give you peace.

God even has a whole chapter in His Book where He expresses that pleasure or approval. You could say He's taking the opportunity to brag on His children!

It's Hebrews chapter 11 and it's full of God's commenda-tions or praises of those who trusted Him and obeyed Him **through faith.**

Zephaniah 3:17 even says, "The Mighty One will save, He rejoices over us with gladness, and He will quiet you with His love, He will even rejoice over you with singing!"

Let your imagination go with me for just a second for this next thought. If God had a phone and a selfie stick, then these snippets in Hebrews 11 would be the pictures He would have taken. Each section of scriptures are like pictures of what people did TOGETHER with HIM! With that being said, He has pictures or memories on His phone with you too! Pictures of things you have done together **through faith.**

When you trust and obey, which is having faith, you're simply recognizing that God has the leading role in the relationship. He leads and you follow. When you see that God is seeking true worshippers you can now understand that He's initiating and leading in the relationship.

Since you're a member of the bride of Christ who is in a covenant relationship with Jesus, then that makes Him the husband right? The Bible says, "He who finds a wife finds a good thing and obtains favor from the Lord"

(Proverbs 18:22). It doesn't say, "She who finds a good husband." Again, who's choosing whom? Who is leading in the relationship? You or Him? It's pretty clear that He is the Author and Finisher of our faith and of our worship!

Now let's go back again to the origin of worship, at least the first time the word is used in the Bible and see what we can learn. **As always, we can learn a lot from studying the original.** The first time the word *worship* is used in the Bible gives us the clearest and most pure definition of worship. Bible scholars call this the law of first mention. This is another great tool in biblical interpretation, along with context and letting the Bible interpret itself.

Let's read from Genesis 22 and learn from the life of Abraham and Isaac. Abraham is the man Paul called "the father of our faith" (Romans 4:12-16). This is a long scripture passage so please read slowly and prayerfully. Read it with fresh eyes, I like to say.

> *"Now it came to pass after these things that God tested Abraham, and said to him, 'Abraham!' And he said, 'Here I am.' Then He said, 'Take now your son, your only son Isaac, whom you love, and go to the land of Moriah, and offer him there as a burnt offering on one of the*

mountains of which I shall tell you.' So, Abraham rose early in the morning and saddled his donkey, and took two of his young men with him, and Isaac his son; and he split the wood for the burnt offering and arose and went to the place of which God had told him. Then on the third day Abraham lifted his eyes and saw the place afar off. And Abraham said to his young men, **'Stay here with the donkey; the lad and I will go yonder and worship, and we will come back to you.'** *So, Abraham took the wood for the burnt offering and laid it on Isaac his son; and he took the fire in his hand, and a knife, and the two of them went together. But Isaac spoke to Abraham his father and said, 'My father!' And he said, 'Here I am, my son.' Then he said, 'Look, the fire, and the wood, but where is the lamb for a burnt offering?' And Abraham said, 'My son, God will provide for Himself the lamb for a burnt offering.' So, the two of them went together. Then they came to the place of which God had told him. And Abraham built an altar there and placed the wood in order; and he bound Isaac his son and laid him on* the altar, upon the wood. And Abraham stretched out his hand and took the knife to slay his son. But the Angel of the Lord called to him from heaven and said, 'Abraham, Abraham!' So, he said, 'Here I am.' And He said, 'Do not lay your hand on the lad, or do anything to him; for now, I know that you fear God, since you have not withheld your son, your only son, from Me.' Then Abraham lifted his eyes and looked, and there behind him was a ram caught in a thicket by its horns. So, Abraham went and took the ram, and offered it up for a burnt offering instead of his son. And Abraham called the name of the place, The-Lord-Will-Provide; as it is said to this day, 'In the Mount of the Lord it shall be provided.' Then the Angel of the Lord called to Abraham a second time out of heaven, and said: 'By Myself I have sworn, says the Lord, because you have done this thing, and have not withheld your son, your only son—blessing I will bless you, and multiplying I will multiply your descendants as the stars of the heaven and as the sand which is on the seashore; and your descendants shall possess the gate of their enemies. In your seed all the nations of the earth shall be blessed, because you have obeyed My voice.'"

Genesis 22:1–18

This chapter contains such rich treasure in regard to understanding the life of Jesus, the love of the Father, the Mission of Love, and your place with Him! This chapter reveals covenant intimacy, agreement, and partnership! This is the first time the word worship is used in the Bible and this chapter is the very root of Family Mission.

There are so many Christians today trying to claim and walk in the blessing of Abraham. **You cannot separate the blessing of Abraham from the trust, obedience, and worship of Abraham!** Since Abraham is called the father of your faith, I think it would really benefit you to see His faith or trust in action. Again, God commends or brags on his faith and that of many others in Hebrews chapter 11.

The Genesis 22 account is mentioned in Hebrews 11:17-19:

> *"By faith Abraham, when he was tested, offered up Isaac, and he who had received the promises offered up his only begotten son, of whom it was said, 'In Isaac your seed shall be called,' concluding that God was able to raise him up, even from the dead, from which he also received him in a figurative sense."*

Many Christians today have come to understand that God wants them blessed. They see the blessing of Abraham belonging to them as promised in Galatians 3:13-14,29:

"Christ has redeemed us from the curse of the law, having become a curse for us (for it is written, 'Cursed is everyone who hangs on a tree'), that the blessing of Abraham might come upon the Gentiles in Christ Jesus, that we might receive the promise of the Spirit through faith. And if you are Christ's, then you are Abraham's seed, and heirs according to the promise."

Yet let's be honest and admit many struggles to see this blessing manifested in their lives. Let me emphasize again this truth. **You cannot separate the blessing of Abraham from his trust and obedience. You cannot separate the blessing of Abraham from the life of WORSHIP you see in Abraham!**

Far too often the trend is to change what you believe to suit your circumstances rather than hold to your beliefs and trust God in relationship to change the circumstances. Jesus is the Word made flesh (John 1:14). The Word of God is clearly His will. So, in no uncertain terms, **Jesus is Perfect Theology!**

I think the problem is often that people like to see themselves as the exception to the rule. Many times, the problem can be a hurtful and even a prideful disposition. As a pastor, I've seen the enemy play on this attitude or disposition time and time again. When people see someone else being blessed, they feel like they're on the outside looking in, instead of rejoicing with those who rejoice. Or they see things going along for years or even decades with nothing changing and no increase in their lives. Then the enemy tries to make them feel like the black sheep of the family.

NO, NO, NO! You are not the rejected one; you are the accepted one. You're not the exception to the rule or promise of blessing; you're right in line. You're in Christ and Christ is in you. There is plenty of power and blessing for all of God's children to be BLESSED, BLESSED, BLESSED! So, say this out loud with me right now:

Jesus is perfect theology.

If I see it in the life of Jesus, then I can see it in my life.

If I see it in the life of Abraham, then I can see it in my life.

The blessing of Abraham came upon me when I entered into covenant union and relationship with Christ Jesus.

Jesus is perfect theology

Instead of changing what you believe or trying to make some theological exception in your life, **let's learn from a real-life Family Mission-** the lives of Abraham, Sarah, and Isaac. Let me draw your attention to a few key verses in Genesis 22.

Verse 16 says, *"because you have done this thing, and have not withheld your son, your only son— blessing I will bless you, and multiplying I will multiply your descendants as the stars of Heaven and as the sand which is on the seashore; and your descendants will possess the gate of their enemies."*

You cannot claim the faith of Abraham as something that stands alone. Faith is entirely relational. You cannot claim to be a true worshipper without understanding what is taking place in this chapter. **The blessing of Abraham and his worship came out of a faith that held nothing back from God. That's a place of worship that Jesus prepared for us!**

Abraham, Sarah, and Isaac were a family walking out steps of obedience! Obedience requires trust! Don't let that be too simple. As I've been saying over and over, faith is another word for trust. Trust is a relationship word; it's not a religious word. Trust is a worship word. Nothing is really going to flow from all that He is and all that He has until He has our complete trust and obedience!

That is what real worship looks like! That's a real place of worship! I think sometimes it's not been understood what happened in the Garden of Eden. We talked about this briefly in the last chapter. Yes, man sinned but what's worse is that **a Father lost the trust of His son.** This helps us understand what Jesus was helping us to see. What does it look like when a son perfectly trusts and obeys His Father? What does it look like to remain in the place of submission to love? Under the Mission of Love? Just like the rich young ruler in Jesus' day recorded in Mark 10. God knows what to ask in order to test your trust. He's not testing you to be cruel. He wants you to work with Him. **He wants you to discover where your heart really is.** He wants to remove any barrier to intimacy, agreement, and partnership!

God knows what to ask to test your trust.

He wants to remove all barriers to intimacy, agreement, and partnership!

It's so easy to learn the language and Christian ways made popular by the Christian Pop Culture! We have done mission work in other nations. We always try to learn the language as much as possible to make a heart connection. However just because I learn the French language doesn't make me French! Just because you learn Christian language and expressions doesn't make you a true worshipper. He wants to entrust His precious things to you. He wants you to be a child who can be entrusted with bigger and bigger portions of the family mission. A mission that goes way beyond the few years of this life.

Testing really is all about promotion; it's about reward. Unfortunately, many people today do not believe that God tests us. The Bible speaks of the TRIAL of your faith being much more precious than gold! (I Peter 1:7) Think about how people see money or gold as so precious today. Consider the effort and extremes people go through to get the gold to purchase what they want in their life. **It is sad that many do not have a correct eternal perspective to understand that the trial and approval of faith is of utmost importance to God!** It's of utmost value to Him and should be to you as well.

I heard it said this way one time, "God's greatest pain is to be doubted and His greatest joy is to be trusted!"

It gives Him joy to work with you and have you work with Him. My wife and I have two adult sons. There's hardly a greater joy than working with them. Yes, we play together and enjoy recreation, but oh, the joy and satisfaction of working with them. Just being with them. Teaching them and learning together with them is such a rich experience!

Yes, it's important for you to trust God, but here's a good question. Can you be trusted? Now it's no mystery why the devil works to get people so confused about trials or tribulations in this life. Whether it's God testing your trust and obedience through instructions or circumstances putting pressure on you, both reveal your level of trust and both are of the utmost importance to God. Sometimes I go through difficulty and trials in life because of my choices or the choices of others. It's not God testing me, but it is a test of my faith none the less!

Abraham's trust in God was revealed on that mountain. In Genesis 22:5, Abraham knows what He is about to do. His trust and obedience to God means he is going to put his son to death as a sacrifice. It doesn't end there; this is supposed to be a burnt offering! Wait! What? That's right; but his obedience also includes him seeing God raise Isaac from the dead. Faith is not only trust; it's linked to vision! Abraham had to see his only begotten son raised up from the ashes! Remember, this is the son about whom God made promises to Abraham regarding a legacy. A legacy so big that it was like numbering the stars of the sky or the grains of sand on the seashore (Genesis 15:5,6).

Hebrews 11:17-19 tells us more about Abraham's faith for a resurrection. It says, *"By faith Abraham, when he was tested, offered up Isaac, and he who had received the promises offered up his only begotten son (Does that sound familiar?) of whom it was said, 'in Isaac your seed shall be called,'* **concluding that God was able to raise him up, even from the dead, from which he also received him is a figurative sense."**

The word *figurative* is in the NKJV, but the literal Hebrew is "figure." We get our word *vision* from the root of this same word. You will see in Genesis 22:4 that *"on the third day— Abraham lifted up his eyes and saw* **the place** *from afar."* Yes, he saw the physical place God wanted him to build the altar, but according to Hebrews 11 he saw more than that. Remember you can only have faith and trust God based on what He has said or revealed to you (allowed you to SEE).

Remember that your place with God is one where He reveals Himself and makes Himself real. If Abraham was going to trust God for a resurrection from the dead, even up from the ashes, then he needed a word, a revelation, or a vision from God. A vision of God raising an "only begotten son from the dead on the third day." Does any of that sound familiar? Fast forward a couple thousand years. Is there anything that happened in the mountainous land of Moriah on the third day with an only begotten son?

I admit this may only be my interpretation of the possibilities regarding this passage, but I think it's worth considering. I do know this for sure, Abraham and Isaac had to have had faith for a resurrection, otherwise the promise dies here! Remember, faith in God can only come from revelation or vision that God gives by what He says or chooses to reveal through other means. Vision is seeing. We even use this phraseology today. Someone explains something with words, and we say, "Yes, I see that." Well, you didn't physically see it, you inwardly saw it. So, whether Abraham had an inner vision, or he saw into the future as a Prophet, he had faith in God for a resurrection after seeing A PLACE afar off on the third day. Notice Abraham's words again, *"I and the lad will go yonder and WORSHIP, and **we will return again!"***

Let's take a look at some further evidence. Consider Isaac's role in this! Isaac's part in this is a powerful ingredient in Family Mission and reviving the Mission of Love! As a young man this was not going to happen unless he was in complete agreement and willing to partner with Abraham his father. Remember, worship is about intimacy, agreement, and partnership. How could Abraham get his son Isaac in agreement? How could He get him to partner with him? What level of intimacy would have authored such trust in Isaac?

On one hand, Isaac certainly could have trusted the faith of his father by just the virtue of the fact he was born. His birth was a miraculous birth for sure! Abraham and Sarah trusted God's Word and vision of legacy to have their only begotten son. Maybe that was enough? Perhaps though, Abraham was able to explain what he saw in a vision or through some other form of revelation?

This we do know for sure, Isaac was in **a place** of agreement, otherwise he could have easily overpowered his father. As a son he was a willing covenant partner! Otherwise, he would simply have said, "Forget this, dad! I think you've taken the faith in God thing a little too far! You're not the one dying here after all." Isaac could have easily reasoned this one away. Allow me a little liberty here. Perhaps he did ask. **"Father, is there any other way?"** Does that question sound familiar? Maybe Isaac said, "Nevertheless, not my will but your will be done!" Do those words sound familiar too? This is a place of true worship! This is intimacy, agreement, and partnership. Even though we can't be certain of the conversation we can be certain this is one of the most prophetic types and shadows of Christ and His Father.

This leads into another perspective that sheds light on this precious passage! Jesus, as a son, found His life, identity, and purpose in the Word of God, the Torah he read and studied as a young Jewish boy. You also will find your value, identity, and purpose in the Word of God. Real worship songs will feed these realities! The life of Isaac and the life of Joseph are very revealing along these lines. Of course, Noah, David, Daniel, and many others have light to shine as well. Isaac and Joseph are especially enlightening. Much more about Joseph in an upcoming chapter.

Joseph knew his life was to deliver the lives of his brothers and family! Jesus knew His life was to deliver the lives of His brothers and family. Abraham and Isaac undoubtedly gave Jesus clarity of what His life was all about. Jesus spoke of it repeatedly by saying that He was going to die, but on the third day He would rise from the dead! He said it so often that in the sixteenth chapter of Matthew, Peter tried to rebuke Him and told Him to quit talking that way!

Jesus then turned and rebuked Peter and said, "You don't understand the things of God and what spirit is influencing you." It was then that Jesus explained that, like a kernel of corn, unless He planted His life in death, He would have no chance of bringing many sons to glory! Did you catch that? He knew His life would bring many sons to glory! **You cannot have a harvest without seed!** When you understand **a place** of worship as seen in Genesis 22 and the life of Jesus, then you will also be able to savor the things of God. You will **see the power of a life perfectly submitted to the Mission of Love!** A life that is lived as a seed!

When Jesus said follow Me, He was inviting you into a life of true worship. He is inviting you into a life of intimacy, agreement, and partnership with the Father as well. Then and only then can you be inspired and equipped to remain in His love as Jesus remained in **the place** of His Father's love (John 15:10). Worship is really working in covenant love with God and others to accomplish His plan and His purpose.

I like to say it this way, according to Genesis 22, worship is covenant families working together in covenant love fulfilling covenant Kingdom purposes! Your true worship has meaning and impact now in this age, but also in the age to come. **Love has a mission.** You are privileged to be given **a place** in it. Certainly, you and I do not understand everything about this, but we understand enough to keep searching. Enough to keep reaching. Enough to keep trusting. Enough to keep worshipping!

It's important that you select songs of worship that nurture and strengthen these holy truths. It's important that we arrange our worship gatherings to nurture and strengthen these holy truths. It's important that we worship in our homes as families to nurture and strengthen these holy truths!

Worship is covenant families working together in covenant love fulfilling covenant Kingdom purposes!

Life in the Mansion

Let's continue our journey further into the very heart and core of this book and the assignment upon it. That's right, this book is a journey together and it is a Kingdom assignment. Let's begin by looking into some extremely important chapters of the Bible: John chapters 13-17. These chapters are essential in understanding the family mission of Jesus. They are foundational in understanding the Divine Reset accomplished by Jesus. In these chapters Jesus is going to share His final thoughts before He goes to the cross as the Lamb of God. As the Lamb of God, He will take away the sins of the world.

These chapters record an intense time of focus regarding the passionate pursuit of His life! These are the final moments of a family mission that was prophesied by John the Baptist in John 1:29,36, "Behold the Lamb of God who takes away the sin of the world." As we've previously seen,

Genesis 22 is a prophetic foreshadowing of this very night, and the family mission Jesus was on. In Genesis 22, Abraham and Isaac represent our Father and our Lord working together in covenant love and covenant purpose. Perfectly mirroring that event, now Jesus is working with the Father to redeem His family and the plan of God for man through the Mission of Love.

As we've said before, **the Bible is actually a story about an eternal family mission!** These 5 chapters in John unveil and explain this Mission of Love. This evening takes place during the Feast of Passover. Look first please at John 14:1-3, *"Let not your heart be troubled; you believe in God, believe also in Me. In My Father's house are many **mansions**; if it were not so, I would have told you. I go to prepare **a place for you.** And if I go and prepare **a place for you**, I will come again and receive you to Myself; that **where I am, there you may be also**."*

A PLACE FOR YOU! Did you know that is why Jesus came? Did you know that was "the joy set before Him" that gave Him the strength to endure all the suffering of the Cross? (Hebrews 12:2) Not only the physical aspects, but the emotional and spiritual dimensions as well?

**A place being prepared for you and me
was what it was all about!**

A place that was lost by the first Adam and is fully restored by the last Adam. It's almost the entire focus of His prayer in John 17. It's vital to recognize that everything He talked with His disciples about in chapters 13-16 He prayed out in chapter 17! Please get ready for a great shift and updraft in your soul. What you're about to read is not intended to take something from you, but rather to impart something into you.

It all begins in verse 2 of chapter 14. Unfortunately, the word *mansions* in verse 2 has actually limited the scope and impact of Jesus' words here. When we hear *mansions,* we often think of great and stately estate homes that we will receive when we get to Heaven. Many times, these verses are shared at funerals to comfort and encourage the heart of mourners regarding the life to come. And there's nothing wrong with that! But please stay with me as we search this out together.

One of the most important lessons I've learned as a follower of Christ and a Bible believing child of God is that we need to always let the Bible interpret the Bible. Before we let man try to explain it, we need to let it explain itself! The Greek word for _mansions_ found in verse 2 is the same word translated _home_ in verse 23. According to Strong's Exhaustive Concordances,

John chapter 14, verses 2 and 23 are the only two times this word is used in the entire New Testament. It's the word *mone*, which is Strong's word 3438.

In addition to letting the Bible interpret itself you need to keep scriptures in context. In Bible school they said context is king! The most powerful revelation and application of any scripture is going to be in its context. Many scriptures do reveal principles and precedents that reach beyond the context, but again, the richest revelation and application of any scripture is going to be in its context.

When Jesus talked about going away to prepare **a place** and then coming again to receive you, was He just talking about going to Heaven when you die? Was He just talking about having a fancy house or estate over in glory? It will be exciting to say the least to walk the streets of gold and see the gates of pearl. I'm sure we will be picking our faces up off the ground as we see it for the first time. The walls of precious stone that surround the city of God will be breathtaking. There is no doubt our accommodations will be stunning. However, when Jesus spoke of **the place** that would be prepared for us, He was not speaking of a mansion in the way most have thought.

Yes, it's going to be glorious on the other side of the door called death. But a person would have to ignore virtually everything else Jesus said in John chapters 13-17 to conclude that He was only talking about a physical mansion or home! Even a simple word study with a reputable concordance, like Strong's or Thayer's, challenges that common conclusion. **The place** He is referring to will impact your life in ways that will be hard to define in such temporal or physical terms!

Let's look again at verse 23 where He used the same Greek word as in verse two, translated *mansion*. "*Jesus answered and said to him, 'If anyone loves Me, he will keep My word; and My Father will love him, and We will come to him and* **make Our _home_ with him**.*'*" Notice how He described **the place** He was preparing. He said with us and in us. Whoa! **<u>Now that changes everything.</u>**

Verse 23 is actually an answer to a question in verse 22 where Judas asked Him how He could manifest Himself to His followers and not to the world. The Amplified translation of verse 22 refers to Jesus *revealing* Himself and making Himself *real* to the disciples and not to the world! Jesus said He would reveal Himself and make Himself real to you. Glory to God. This is **the place** that was prepared for you! **A place** where our Heavenly Father and the Lord Jesus will be *revealed* to you and made very *real* to you!

A place made possible by the work and communion of the Holy Spirit. Jesus speaks of this for almost the entire sixteenth chapter of John. Let's look at a few verses just to touch on this.

> *Jesus said, "I still have many things to say to you, **but you cannot bear them now.** However, when He, the Spirit of truth, has come, He will guide you into all truth; for He will not speak on His own authority, but whatever He hears He will speak; and He will tell you things to come. He will glorify Me, for He will take of what is Mine and declare it to you. All things that the Father has are Mine. Therefore, I said that He will take of Mine and declare it to you."*

John 16:12-15

Jesus had many things to say but couldn't until the Holy Spirit had come. Notice verse 15, "All things that the Father has are Mine. Therefore, I said that He will take of Mine and declare it to you." Please don't let that statement just sail past you. That is a truly mansion-sized truth, especially when you read it from the Amplified Bible.

"Everything that the Father has is Mine. That

is what I meant when I said that He [the Spirit] will take the things that are Mine and will **reveal (declare, disclose, transmit) it to you.** *"*

John 16:15 AMPC

Wow! <u>What an amazing place He prepared for you!</u> **Declare! Disclose! Transmit!** We might as well add one more that we all understand. **Download!** Have you ever had a *Download* from Heaven? If so, then you are living proof that God was communicating wirelessly long before our technology caught up with Him. Let's look again at this mansion-sized truth Jesus just released.

A place where you can have access to all things the Father has. **A place** where all things can be revealed, declared, disclosed, transmitted, and DOWNLOADED! It's **a place** of authority and dominion! It's **a place** of binding and loosing (Matthew 16:19). If that's not a mansion-sized truth affecting how and where you live, then what is? Jesus said it this way in another place. It is the Father's good pleasure to give us the Kingdom (Luke 12:32). Jesus said the Kingdom is within us (Luke 17:21)!

Colossians 1:26,27 in the Passion Translation is simply marvelous.

"There is a divine mystery—a secret surprise

that has been concealed from the world for generations, but now it's being revealed, unfolded and manifested for every holy believer to experience. Living within you is the Christ who floods you with the expectation of glory! This mystery of Christ, embedded within us, becomes a heavenly treasure chest of hope filled with the riches of glory for his people, and God wants everyone to know it!"

However, let's stay focused for now on these chapters in John. You can see this is not an isolated idea, but a thread of truth that runs through all of the New Testament epistles. This is much of the mystery I referred to in chapter one. In the fifteenth chapter of John, Jesus talks about Him being the vine and you being the branches that would bear the fruit, specifically the fruit of relationship and your communion in prayer! He spoke of abiding, or living, in Him and His words in you and then you could ask whatever you wanted, and it would be done unto you (John 15:7)! John 15:10 also highlights **the place** that He prepared for you.

*"If you keep My commandments, you will **abide in My love**, just as I have kept My Father's commandments and **abide in His love**."*

The place prepared for you is a place for you to live in or abide in. It's a place where you and I are living and abiding in the Love of God our Father! A place where you could ask for what you desire, and it would be granted to you. Sounds like a mansion to me!

Now let's look at perhaps the most powerful confirmation regarding **the place** He was preparing for you! In John 17, Jesus is praying for us specifically! This prayer is the wrap up of the entire discourse from John 13-17. In John 17:3, Jesus says eternal life is knowing God, and not just knowing about Him. Sounds like Him revealing Himself and being real to you! Again, the Passion Translation of this verse is exceptional.

> *"Eternal life means to **know and experience** you as the only true God, and to **know and experience** Jesus Christ, as the Son whom you have sent."*

John 17:3 TPT

Knowing and experiencing your Father and your Lord Jesus Christ! That's eternal life. That's living large! In fact, in this prayer, Jesus said, "that they..." ten different times. "That" is a word that expresses effect, consequence, or result. He was very intentional in this prayer and so should you be! Jesus knew exactly what the effect, consequence, or result of His life planted in faith would be.

Now let's jump on down in His prayer to verse 20,

> *"I do not pray for these alone, but also **for those who will believe in Me through their word;** that they all may be one, as You, Father, are in Me, and I in You; that they also may be one in Us, **that the world may believe that You sent Me.** And the glory which You gave Me I have given them, that they may be one just as We are one: I in them, and You in Me; that they may be made perfect in one, and **that the world may know that You have sent Me, and have loved them as You have loved Me.** Father, I desire that they also whom You gave Me may be with Me where I am, that they may behold My glory which You have given Me; for You loved Me before the foundation of the world."*

John 17:20-24

Notice in verse 20 He is praying for all of us who have believed on Him through their testimony as Apostles of the Lamb! That's us for sure. We have faith in Jesus today through the scriptures they provided us as well as the anointed preaching and teaching of those scriptures. But brace yourself as we look further, specifically at what He asked the Father in this prayer. It has everything to do with **the place** that He knew was being prepared for you through His death, burial, resurrection, and ascension.

It's **a place** man had with God from the beginning.

It's **a place** that was lost and it's **a place** that Jesus came to restore!

I like to say it this way at Family Mission. Jesus accomplished a Divine Reset! So, are you ready? Here we go. He asked the Father in verse 21, "**that they all may be one, as You, Father, are in Me, and I in You, that they also may be one in Us!**" Oh, my goodness, did you catch that?

That is what you call GOOD NEWS. That is what you call THE GOSPEL. *You see the gospel is the Good News of **a place** that man lost being fully restored.* A oneness and walk with God that was lost being fully restored! An intimacy that man had with God that was lost and was fully restored! An agreement that man had with God being fully restored. A partnership that man had with God being fully restored.

Jesus said it again immediately so there can be no mistake about His intentions or His mission. In verse 22 and 23 He said, "*And the glory which You gave Me I have given* them, ***that they may be one just as We are one: I in them, and You in Me; that they may be made perfect in one,*** *and that the world may know that You have sent Me and* ***have loved them as You have loved Me."*** Jesus said this oneness and grand intimacy would be the key factor in the world believing He was sent by the Father.

Again, Heaven is going to be amazing, and your dwelling there will be incredible for sure. BUT what Jesus just explained in John chapters 13-17 was more incredible than you and I dying and going to Heaven one day. The Gospel of the Lord Jesus Christ is the forgiveness of sins so that **a place** could be prepared for you and me. So that a place could be restored for all mankind to receive. They just need to hear, but how can they hear unless someone tell them?

A place of intimacy and oneness with God. **A place** of communion and fellowship with God. **A place** you can move into, and He can move into the moment you've made Jesus the Lord and Savior of your life. Sounds to me like **we are now a place for Heaven's glory to abide.** After all, what makes Heaven so awesome? It's Him! Remember verse 23 of John 14. "*Jesus answered and said to him, 'If anyone loves Me, he will keep My word; and My Father will love him, and We will come to him and make Our* ***home*** *with him.'*" Your mansion in Him!

When we believe the Gospel as Jesus intended, we should feel like we just moved into a mansion because we have! We become a walking habitation of God! That's one awesome mobile home if you ask me! Paul brought this revelation by the Holy Spirit just like Jesus said it would happen in John 16:13.

"And what agreement has the temple of God with idols? ***For you are the temple of the living God.*** *As God has said:* ***'I will dwell in them and walk among them.*** *I will be their God, and they shall be My people.' Therefore 'Come out from among them and be separate, says the Lord. Do not touch what is unclean, And I will receive you.* ***I will be a Father to you, And you shall be My sons and daughters,'*** *Says the LORD Almighty." II Corinthians 6:16-18*

When you believe and receive the Gospel, then you move into **the place He prepared for you!** You move into **the place** that the first Adam lost, but **the place** the last Adam restored. In Colossians 1:6TPT Paul calls it the astonishing revelation of the Gospel.

"For [the ceremonies] deal only with clean and unclean meats and drinks and different washings, [mere] external rules and regulations for the body imposed to tide the worshipers over until ***the time of setting things straight [of***

*reformation, of **the complete new order** when Christ, the Messiah, shall establish **the reali-ty** of what these things foreshadow–a better covenant]."*

Hebrews 9:10 AMPC.

Jesus had reformation on His mind long before any known reformers of our day. A better covenant means a better **place** with God. A better and more intimate relation-ship with Him! I am so thankful for Jesus showing us what it looks like for a man to walk with God the Father and to remain in His Love (John 15:10). I am so thankful that **He set things straight and established the reality of all the old covenant foreshadowed!**

We can all agree on how twisted mankind has become over the last few thousand years. How we treat each other has become twisted. You've got to be careful not to study a fallen man to understand who you are! Study Jesus to understand who you really are and who you're called to be. Thank God Jesus set things straight and prepared **a place for you!** He restored the place that man had with God which was lost and then got so twisted up! It would be greatly advantageous now to read John 13-17 with the understanding that there is **a place prepared for you**.

A place for you to walk with God just like Jesus walked with God. **A place** for you to have a reputation in prayer just like Jesus had in prayer. **A place** where your life is so transformed that you are conformed into the image of the Son of God (Romans 8:29).

A place where nothing can steal your peace or diminish your joy.

A place where it's more blessed to give than to receive.

A place where your life is like a city on a hill that cannot be hidden.

A place where your value, identity and purpose are re-set to their original settings!

A place where you bear the image of the Heavenly Man and not just the image of the man of dust (I Corinthians 15:49).

Sounds to me like you have an amazing mansion waiting on you to move in. Are you ready? The question is, are you ready for God the Father and God the Son to move in? (John 14:23) In Romans 8 it says the world is groaning and in travail waiting for the manifestation of the sons of God. That's sons who have moved into their mansion!

Philemon 6 in the Laubach Translation says it best: *"I pray that everyone who meets you would catch your faith and learn how wonderful it is to live in Christ Jesus!"*

If you're willing to accept what Jesus was teaching and praying in John 13-17 then we would like to say, "Welcome home to your new mansion!" You're back where you've always belonged from the beginning.

In Luke 15 Jesus furthers His teaching along these lines when He tells a trilogy of stories about something, or someone lost. What is the definition of something, or someone lost? One simple definition is they are not where they belong! Jesus went to prepare a place for us because none of us were where we belonged. In Luke 15 He talked about a lost sheep. He talked about a lost coin. Then He talked about a lost son. All of these were not where they belonged.

In the famous story of the prodigal son coming home here's what the Father said as He celebrated and welcomed His son home; *"It was right that we should make merry and be glad, for your brother was dead and is alive again, and was lost and is found.* «He's back where he belongs! The Father put a ring back on his finger. He put the best robe on his back. He put shoes back on his feet. He then said something to the eldest son that will rock your world. The father was answering his eldest son's complaint of the father never giving him anything! Here's what the father replied, "Son why are you saying such a thing? All that I have is yours!" Did you hear that? ALL THAT I HAVE IS YOURS!

That's the place Jesus was preparing. A place with Him in God where all that the Father has is yours. Now that's a MANSION. You can see now why the enemy wants you to simply sing about a mansion over in glory one day instead of moving into a place with Christ in God today! When you say yes to Jesus and all that He accomplished in His death, burial, resurrection, and ascension then you have come home in your heart. Welcome home.

II Corinthians chapter 3 provides a great key to moving into your mansion. It's a great key to actually living in **the place** Jesus prepared for you! There are some incredibly profound comparisons and applications made in this chapter. Please take time to read II Corinthians 3. Pause and do it now if you can.

Paul, who understood the mystery and **the place,** is comparing the old and new covenants. He is actually comparing the glory of these covenants. He is comparing the ministry of death, written, and engraved on stones, to the ministry of the Spirit. He is comparing the ministry of condemnation to the ministry of righteousness. Paul says at the beginning of the chapter that we have been made able ministers of the new covenant, of the Spirit and of life!

Let's confess that right now together, **"I have been made an able minister of the new covenant, of the Spirit and of life! I live and abide in the place that Jesus prepared for me"** Paul was a man who clearly understood this mystery and **the place** Jesus prepared for you! He said the glory that is in our lives as born-again Christians is so much greater that if laid side by side, would completely eclipse the glory on the life of Moses. Selah … Pause in His presence … Let that sink in!

Let's trust Holy Spirit to continue renewing our minds to think in line with the word of God and the mind of Christ. At the end of II Corinthians chapter 3 Paul talks about a veil being taken away in Christ. This is prophetically and practically fulfilled in the incredible miracle that took place when Jesus cried out on Calvary and breathed out His last breath. The Bible records a great earthquake happening and the veil was torn in the Temple from top to bottom (Mark 15:37,38).

What's so significant about that, you may ask? Before this moment, only one man once a year went into the presence of God behind that veil. It was the High Priest on the day of Atonement. The veil being torn, and the blood of Jesus being shed means that now, anyone who believes and trusts in Jesus, and in the Gospel, can stand in the presence of God without guilt, shame, or condemnation! (Colossians 1:22) **Glory to God! What a place! A place with God; without guilt, shame, or condemnation.**

What an invitation! What a mansion! Think with me how much your life would change if you really believed and walked in the light of righteousness. Romans 5:17 says it this way, *"those who receive the abundance of grace and of the gift of righteousness will **reign in this life** through one Jesus Christ."* Reigning in life sounds pretty good, doesn't it?

That's **a place** of dominion. That's not being on the bottom. That's being on the top. In fact, the best way to understand the word *repent* is to return to the top! Pent is the root of penthouse or the top house. Jesus preached repent because He wanted us to return to the top. He was preparing **a place** for man back at the top, where mankind fell from in the Garden of Eden. We need to make sure we fully understand what ruling and reigning in this life looks like.

Simply put, IT LOOKS JUST LIKE JESUS!

It looks like a man who showed you how to remain or live in the love of His Father. It looks like a man who was willing to lay His life down. It looks like a man who walked on water and paid taxes after a day of fishing. It looks like a man who brought a touch of healing and deliverance everywhere He went. It looks like a man who took care of His mother with the last few breaths of His life on earth. It looks like a man whose words sounded different than others who had been teaching about God. It looks like a man who was full of Love and NEVER in NEED of Love because He was Love in the flesh.

This is why Jesus is called the King of Kings and the Lord of Lords! As you take up your cross (the Mission of Love) you will live a life of complete dominion and authority. There will be no place for you to hide. There will be no place for you to keep a low profile. Light exposes the darkness. Light removes the darkness. In Ephesians 5:8 Paul says we are light in the Lord. He tells us to walk as children of light! God is Love and God is Light, and God is Holy! (I John 1:5; 4:16 & I Peter 1:16)

These are not competing realities but harmonious realities! Sounds like your mansion is **a place** in the light! He also says in Ephesians 5:1 to imitate God like a dear child. This is both simple and powerful!

Now back to II Corinthians 3. Paul concluded by telling you to behold as in a mirror the glory of the Lord with an unveiled face! Like a groom who lifts the veil to kiss his bride for the very first time, let the Holy Spirit **reset** your innocence before the Lord and have Holy Communion with Him. Please don't let this be weird, but let it open up your heart so the King of Glory can fully enter in.

It's sad that the enemy has corrupted our society and polluted covenant intimacy that these amazing truths can't even be preached or taught like they should. We, however, refuse to hold back from revealing and unveiling the mystery of the Gospel. Refuse to hold back from fully proclaiming and explaining **the place He prepared for us!**

Next time you take Holy Communion give the Holy Spirit the opportunity to **reset** your innocence in the presence of the Lord. Let the Father put the robe on you. Let the Father put the ring on your finger. Let the Father put shoes back on your feet. Let the Father tell you, "All that I have is yours!" Let Him remove all shame, guilt, and condemnation. Thank Him for helping you to understand what Paul was talking about in Ephesians 5:31-33 when he said, "This is a great mystery (regarding marriage), but I'm speaking about Christ and the Church."

Jesus said that what God shows you and tells you in secret He wants to demonstrate in the open. That's exactly what Jesus' life was; it was living proof that a man could be intimate with God. It was living proof that a man could walk with God like Adam did in the beginning! Paul finishes in II Corinthians 3 by saying if we will behold His Glory with an unveiled face (no shame, guilt, or condemnation) then we will be transformed or transfigured into the same image from glory to glory, just as by the Spirit of the Lord!

Your mansion with God is a wonderful **place** where you can go from glory to glory and from faith to faith, going from one level of intimacy to another with your Father. Since the Bible was not written in chapter and verse, we need to finish with the first few verses of chapter 4 of II Corinthians. Verses 3-6 read,

> *"But even if our Gospel is veiled, it is veiled to those who are perishing, whose minds the god of this age has blinded, who do not believe, lest the light of the Gospel of the glory of Christ, who is the image of God, should shine on them. For we do not preach ourselves, but Christ Jesus the Lord, and ourselves your bondservants for Jesus' sake. For it is the God who commanded light to shine out of darkness, who has shone in our hearts to give the light of **the knowledge of the glory of God in the face of Jesus Christ.**"*

Your place is where you see His face!

It's important that you experience and walk in everything the Gospel offers so you can shine and show the way to others. It's important that you move into every dimension and expression of the relationship He prepared for you with the Father.

Every person needs to know that they are invited to experience a relationship with God behind the veil! They need to know that they are invited to take their life back to its divine origin. They too can have a Divine Reset! I close this chapter with a few final verses.

> *"And by the blood of His cross, everything in heaven and earth is brought back to himself— back to its original intent, restored to innocence again! ... You perceive how God sees you in the mirror of the Word ... you see your divine origin."*
>
> **Colossians 1:20 and James 1:24 (TPT)**

> ***"Through wisdom a house (or mansion) is built,*** *And by understanding it is established; By knowledge the rooms are filled With all precious and pleasant riches."*
>
> **Proverbs 24:3-4**

*"**Through skillful and godly Wisdom is a house (a life, a home, a family) built,** and by understanding it is established [on a sound and good foundation], And by knowledge shall its chambers [of every area] be filled with all precious and pleasant riches."*

Proverbs 24:3-4 AMPC

CHAPTER FIVE

The Mission of Love

You might have heard it said some time or another, *"One Word from God will change your life forever!"* Well, it's true. His Words are the building blocks of life. One of my favorite quotes, and we use it all the time at Family Mission, is this one by E.W. Kenyon, *"The genius of Christianity is the ability of God to build Himself into us through His Word so that in our everyday life we live just like the Master!"* There is a scripture in Timothy that was a real game changer for our family and our ministry. The truth in it became a major building block in our lives. This Word brought great clarity and transformation. This is why #TruthThatTransforms and #DivineReset are common hashtags used with Family Mission. Before we look at the verse in Timothy here are a few important thoughts.

Ministry can develop into a lot of different things.

It can go in a lot of different directions. There can be so many different motives in church life and ministry. Money can quickly become a motive. Hurt or betrayal can easily become a motive. Ambition can certainly become a motive. Sadly, ego can become a motive.

These horrific words I heard from someone many years ago reveal to us that ministry has gotten way off course. At a gathering of ministers, I heard someone say, "Pastoring would be great if it wasn't for the people!" It's tragic that I ever heard those words spoken. Truly some of the saddest words, but they came out of obvious discouragement. They came out of disappointment. They came out of feelings of hurt and betrayal.

This same frustration with people can develop in any person's life, not just a minister. These are the very same feelings that destroy marriages and families all the time. Many Christians seem to be powerless to overcome in the midst of difficult, toxic, or even abusive relationships.

Jesus was not a hurting minister! Jesus didn't need a sabbatical. Yes, there are times you will need to rest, but not because you want to escape frustration and hurt. God is not seeking worshippers because He needs a boost of encouragement! You don't seek rest just because you're tired of dealing with people. I think we need to learn of Him.

Look at the load He was carrying and yet He said, "Learn of Me: my yoke is easy, and my burden is light" (Matthew 11). This is not a whimsical thought, but a life changing shift. Learning from Him on how to navigate relationships and responsibilities, even difficult relationships, and big responsibilities.

You don't see Jesus throwing down the cross in frustration and disappointment. You don't see Him getting analytical or trying to figure out why people are not understanding Him and then adjusting His message to what they will accept. **He never let what they didn't see change what He did see.** I want to say that again, **He never let what they didn't see change what He did see.** He knew that He just needed to get the Divine seed of love (Agape) in them through faith in the Gospel. He knew if He could get Holy Spirit personally involved in their lives, things would change. He knew if man could just RECEIVE the Holy Spirit (John 20:22), life would be forever transformed back into the original image, back to its original place!

Divine Reset!

Here we go, let's look at I Timothy 1:5-7 in a couple different translations.

New King James Version: *⁵Now the purpose of the*

commandment is love from a pure heart, from a good con-science, and from sincere faith, 6 from which some, having strayed, have turned aside to idle talk, 7 desiring to be teachers of the law, understanding neither what they say nor the things which they affirm.

The Message: *⁵The whole point of what we're un-hinged is simply Love - Love uncontaminated by self-inter-est and counterfeit faith, a life open to God.*

New International Version: ⁵...The goal of the com-mandment is Love...

New Living Translation: ⁵The purpose of my instruction is that all believers would be filled with love that comes from a pure heart, a clear conscience and genuine faith.

Young's Literal Translation: ⁵...The end of the charge is Love...

Jesus came to change the why behind your life. He came to change your view of things. He wanted to change your perspective of people and situations. He wanted to reposition you with a repositioning that would be inward and in the spirit.

**Jesus never let sin against Him excuse
or produce sin in Him.**

Jesus never let what people didn't see change what He did see!

In I Corinthians 13:1-3, the Word of God says that no matter what you do, no matter what you say and understand, no matter what you give and sacrifice, if it's not motivated or fueled by Love, it gains **nothing**! Now think about the things mentioned in I Corinthians 13:1-3. It says if I speak with the tongues of men and of angels, having the gift of prophecy and understanding all mysteries, having all knowledge, having enough faith to move mountains, giving all, I have to feed the poor and giving my life as a martyr. _This would be a Christian superstar by today's standards._ This person's conferences are the ones packed out everywhere they go. Their memorial service is attended by the greatest of the great. Yet God says they may not have gained anything with Him. It's possible that they really weren't a part of His Family Mission: the Mission of Love. It's possible they could have some other motive behind what they did.

The words of Matthew 7:21-23 are sobering. He said many will come to Him in that day talking about all they did in His Name. He then will simply say, "Depart from Me; I never knew you; you workers of iniquity!" Whoa, those are some stunning and powerful words. Jesus' words are never intended to scare you, but they should help keep your focus and motives pure. Purely rooted and grounded in Love!

Love is always seeking reconciliation. Not just seeking to be right. Never forget this: if God comes RIGHT then we are all WRONG. Period. Game over. But the Bible reveals He came seeking reconciliation! He said in Matthew 6:22,23 that if our eye was good or single our whole body would be full of light. That's another way of saying our whole life would be full of light and shining! When we see with an eye or perspective of redemption and reconciliation, it changes everything!

When man fell in the Garden of Eden, he **fell from a place of BEING love to a place of being in NEED of love.** I want to repeat that. Man fell from **a place** of BEING love to **a place** of being in NEED of love! It's absolutely vital for you to understand that. If the Gospel only instructs people that they are loved by God, then they can remain in **a place** of focusing on their need of love. Every relationship will be viewed through that filter! The Gospel should teach people that being born-again through His love for us takes them back to the beginning and puts the very seed of love in them. Love has now re-Fathered them and now they are children of love. They are love. This is a totally different perspective. It begins with being loved and ends with being love!

This is the single or good eye that Jesus was referring to in Matthew 6:22,23. The Gospel is intended to totally change your perspective and the why behind your life. It literally changes your reason for being. This is why Jesus taught us in His famous sermon on the mount the BE AT-TITUDES. I like to call them attitudes of BEING. You no longer wake up for people to treat you right; you wake up to love people! Love is both a place you live from and a purpose for you being alive!

A great promise is attached to having your purpose correct in Romans 8:28. The Bible says that now all things can work out for your good. By the way, **this is the secret to making EVERYDAY A WIN!** Knowing your everyday purpose! Knowing who you really are. Letting your who be the root of all you do. Life is now about who you are and what you are becoming and no longer just about things you need or what's happening to you. From this place in Christ, you actually never again live in a place of fear or worry regarding your needs. When you live in **the place Jesus prepared for you**, you're not in a place of anxiety.

This does not mean you do not have things you need, but it means you have access to all you need through your union with Him! It simply means you've drank the Living Water Jesus offers in John 4:10,13,14 to the Syrophoeni-cian woman. Like her, now you **never thirst again!**

Adam was not in need at all before he sinned! He only experienced being in need once he was separated from God. Adam's identity was love and he was living the Mission of Love on the earth. It was a Family Mission! Adam had work to do, but all his needs were abundantly supplied. Sin reduced him and everyone born after him to being in fear regarding our needs. Man became in need of love and everything else. Why? Because we were separated from God in spirit. This is why you must be born-again. You must be re-Fathered. You must be reconnected or reunited with Love Himself. You must repent and return to the top. You must go back to your original place with the Father!

This is what Jesus was trying to explain in John 15 when He was telling His disciples that He was the vine. You see, Adam was a vine and you are the fruit of that vine, for all have sinned and come short of the glory of God. Jesus came and laid down His life and even said Himself that His life was a seed (John 12:24). He compared it to a grain of wheat, which if planted, would not abide alone but would spring up and bear much fruit. **The death and burial of Jesus was the planting of a new vine.**

A new root was planted you might say! It was to bring forth a new family tree. It was going to be a tree of righteousness, the planting of the Lord (Isaiah 61:1-3).

Jesus said if you make the tree good the fruit will be good (Matthew 12:33). **Jesus makes the tree good. Jesus plants the good seed. He establishes a new root in our lives.** Now through the preaching and teaching of the Gospel we get to seed people's hearts with Love and with righteousness.

Look at what it says in I Corinthians 15:49, *"And as we have borne the image of the man of dust, we shall also bear the image of the Heavenly Man."* Paul brings out this reality and high calling of God in Christ Jesus in Romans 8:29. He tells us that we are destined to be conformed to the image of Christ! **The Gospel calls you to your destiny.** The Gospel invites you to your destiny. The Gospel even reveals how God accomplishes this in your life. He did it by justifying you with the blood of Jesus and then glorified you in your spirit through the regeneration and infilling of the Holy Spirit!

When talking about the Mission of Love, we're really talking about the Great Commission. Remember, it was the Great Commission, and not the Great Suggestion! Remember also, worship is about intimacy, agreement, and **partnership**! It's a Co-Mission!

"And Jesus came and spoke to them, saying,
'All authority has been given to Me in heaven

and on earth. 19 Go therefore and make disciples of all the nations, baptizing them in the name of the Father and of the Son and of the Holy Spirit, 20 teaching them to observe all things that I have commanded you; and lo, I am with you always, even to the end of the age.' Amen."

Matthew 28:18–20

"And He said to them, 'Go into all the world and preach the Gospel to every creature. He who believes and is baptized will be saved; but he who does not believe will be condemned. And these signs will follow those who believe: In My name they will cast out demons; they will speak with new tongues; they will take up serpents; and if they drink anything deadly, it will by no means hurt them; they will lay hands on the sick, and they will recover.' So then, after the Lord had spoken to them, He was received up into heaven, and sat down at the right hand of God. And they went out and preached everywhere, the Lord working with them and confirming the word through the accompanying signs. Amen."

Mark 16:15–20

If you're going to fulfill the Mission of Love or the Great Commission, you need to understand what *the world* means. The Greek word *ethnos* literally means "any order or arrangement of people!" People are certainly ordered and arranged upon the different continents and according to culture or language. However, people are also ordered and arranged around many other things and ideals.

Please consider a thought proposed by others today that society is really ordered and arranged on seven mountains or around seven pillars of influence: Family, Religion/Faith, Education, Business, Government, Media, Arts or Entertainment. It has been said that if you're really going to change the world then you need to conquer these mountains! You need to invade these territories with the Kingdom of God.

When God said in the beginning to replenish the Earth, He was commissioning Adam to re-colonize the Earth with the Kingdom of God. This is a foundational understanding in the advance of the Family Mission.

For far too long we have defined ministry and worship by what happens inside the walls of the assembly, rather than seeing the assembling of ourselves together as having a much higher purpose.

The purpose of assembling is to inspire and equip true worshippers to be that city on a hill (Matthew 5:14). Your purpose is shining the light of the Gospel of the Kingdom in and on these mountains, or territories, of influence. Instead of always trying to bait people to come into the church building, how about we be the church? Be the bait! Philemon 6, in the Laubach translation, says, "I pray that everyone who meets you may catch your faith and learn how wonderful it is to live in Christ Jesus." Faith in God is contagious, and it can spread and be caught!

Some things cannot just be taught, they must be caught! Your life is intended by God to be a light that shines in the darkness. Jesus said, "You are the light of the world, a city that is set on a hill CANNOT be hidden" (Matthew 5:14). Let's make that personal right now and declare it out loud: **I am the light of the World ... I am a city set on a hill!**

If you know who you really are then Jesus said you "cannot be hidden." You will shine! You can't control what people do with the light they see, but you can be sure that they see the light of Christ in your life. The Bible actually calls you a living epistle (II Corinthians 3:2,3). Your life can be God's love letter to your world! You can make sure they see **the treasure** of a life that is one with Him (II Corinthians 4:7).

Consider again these powerful words of Jesus in John 17. He says our oneness with Him and each other is what would cause others to believe in who He is, and that He was sent by the Father.

> *"I do not pray for these alone, but also for those who will believe in Me through their word; that they all may be one, as You, Father, are in Me, and I in You; that they also may be one in Us, **that the world may believe that You sent Me.** And the glory which You gave Me I have given them, that they may be one just as We are one: I in them, and You in Me; that they may be made perfect in one, and **that the world may know that You have sent Me** and have loved them as You have loved Me."*

John 17:20–23

Your life looking just like Jesus is not a man's idea; it's God's idea, and His original intention. It's literally what Jesus prayed for, and I believe He will get His prayers answered. Do you want to be the answer to His prayer? Only you can decide that for you. Will you join Jesus in agreement and thereby be the answer to Jesus' prayer?

This is a huge shift, isn't it? Instead of always thinking about Jesus being the answer to your prayer: you and I can be the answer to His prayer. We could also say it relationally in these terms. It's shifting from trusting God to being trusted by God.

Shifting from trusting God to being trusted by God!

After all He's done for us, the least we could do is say yes to what He's asking. Yes Father, thank you for washing me in the blood of Jesus. Thank you for sending Holy Spirit so that I could receive divine life once again. Thank you for baptizing me in the Holy Spirit and with fire. **Thank you for the incredible place you prepared for me!**

Let's check out what Paul said to the Galatians as we read it in the Message paraphrase. *"It is absolutely clear that God has called you to a free life. Just make sure that you don't use this freedom as an excuse to do whatever you want to do and destroy your freedom. Rather, use your freedom to serve one another in love; **that's how freedom grows.** For everything known about God's Word, it is best summed up in a single sentence: Love others as you love yourself. That's an act of true freedom. If you bite and ravage each other, watch out—in no time at all you will be* *annihilating each other, and where will your precious free-dom be then?"*

That's how freedom grows! That's powerful.

Just like the enemy hijacked the freedom of Adam and Eve in the Garden of Eden, he is still in the hijacking business today. Don't let him define what freedom is. Allow the Author and Giver of life to tell you what true freedom is. Today the enemy attempts to hijack the Gospel because it is the power of God unto salvation to all who believe! (Romans 1:16) He does not want that power released, so he hijacks the meaning of the Gospel from being a message that transforms us into Love into a message that simply benefits us and meets our needs.

Sadly, the enemy has effectively blinded people from the reality that a real Divine Reset occurs when someone is born-again. You're reset to the original settings. You're reset to innocence. You're taken back to the top! You literally get to go back to a place of innocence in the presence of God. You're holy, blameless, and above reproach in His sight, as it says in Colossians, **if indeed** you continue in the faith grounded and steadfast and are not moved away from the hope of the Gospel which you heard (Colossians 1:22,23).

Unfortunately, the enemy of your soul has been

successful at blinding many from that hope and moving yet others away. **You can never forget that you're in a war zone.** As beautiful as this world can be and as advanced as our technology is, we are in a war zone! *"The weapons of your warfare are not carnal, but they are mighty. Mighty in God! For the pulling down of strongholds, casting downs arguments and every high thing that exalts itself above the knowledge of God" (II Corinthians 10).*

If you're going to prevail, you will need to bring every thought into captivity to the obedience of Christ and be ready to punish all disobedience when your obedience is fulfilled (II Corinthians 10:3-6). The seven mountains of influence need to be full of people who are obedient to the Gospel and are ready to shine! Ready and willing to go in a war zone and not retreat but fight to bring people who are blinded and held captive. Help them by showing them a life shining and submitted to the Mission of Love! People need to know that Love is fighting for them, and it will fight till they are found!

Love Is fighting for you.

The unstoppable Love of God is fighting for you.

Love is fighting for families and

Love is fighting for communities.

With this being said, we certainly can consider the lyrics of *Reckless Love*, by Cory Asbury (Bethel Music):

Before I spoke a word, You were singing over me

You have been so, so good to me

Before I took a breath, You breathed Your life in me

You have been so, so kind to me

Oh, the overwhelming, never-ending, reckless love of God

Oh, it chases me down, **fights 'til I'm found**, leaves the ninety-nine

I couldn't earn it, and I don't deserve it, still, You give Yourself away

Oh, the overwhelming, never-ending, reckless love of God, yeah

When I was Your foe, still Your love fought for me

You have been so, so good to me

When I felt no worth, You paid it all for me

But You have been so, so kind to me

There's no shadow You won't light up

Mountain You won't climb up

Coming after me

There's no wall You won't kick down

Lie You won't tear down

Coming after me

Oh, the overwhelming, never-ending, reckless love of God

Oh, it chases me down, fights 'til I'm found, leaves the ninety-nine

And I couldn't earn it, I don't deserve it, still, You give Yourself away

Oh, the overwhelming, never-ending, reckless love of God, yeah.

Another excellent example of God's heart is found in the life of King David, of whom God said, "He is a man after my own heart!" Let's take a look at a low point in King David's life when he and his men lost everything dear and precious to them. Their lives had literally been burnt to the ground. In this prophetic battle at Ziklag, we learn much of the heart of God and our King Jesus. The account is recorded in I Samuel 30:1-8, 18-19, 26:

"Now it happened, when David and his men came to Ziklag, on the third day, that the

Amalekites had invaded the South and Ziklag, attacked Ziklag and burned it with fire, and had taken captive the women and those who were there, from small to great; they did not kill anyone, but carried them away and went their way. So, David and his men came to the city, and there it was, burned with fire; and their wives, their sons, and their daughters had been taken captive. **Then David and the people who were with him lifted up their voices and wept, until they had no more power to weep.** *And David's two wives, Ahinoam the Jezreelitess, and Abigail the widow of Nabal the Carmelite, had been taken captive. Now David was greatly distressed, for the people spoke of stoning him, because the soul of all the people was grieved, every man for his sons and his daughters.* **But David strengthened himself in the Lord his God.** *Then David said to Abiathar the priest, Ahimelech's son, ⟨Please bring the ephod here to me.' And Abiathar brought the ephod to David. So, David inquired of the Lord, saying, ⟨Shall I pursue this troop? Shall I overtake them?' And He answered him,* **'Pursue, for you shall surely overtake them and without** *fail recover all.' So, David recovered all that the Amalekites had carried away, and David rescued his two wives. And nothing of theirs was lacking, either small or great, sons or daughters, spoil, or anything which they had taken from them; David recovered all.* Now when David came to Ziklag, he sent some of the spoil to the elders of Judah, to his friends, saying, ‹Here is a present for you from the spoil of the enemies of the Lord.'"

With the Heavenly Father, His Son King Jesus, and the mighty Holy Spirit fighting for you, I want you to expect to recover all, in the Name of Jesus! King David recovered all. Jesus is called the Son of David! King Jesus has recovered all! You have the privilege of taking this Gospel to your world. As the church, we get to go to every tribe, tongue, people, and nation of the world. But it all starts with your world. So let the heart of the lion of the tribe of Judah roar inside your chest today in Jesus' name!

Having a Redemptive Revelation of God is one of the most important revelations you can receive! This redemptive revelation will draw you to Him and send you out every day as a missionary!

*"Where there is no vision **[no redemptive revelation of God]**, the people perish; but he who keeps the law [of God, which includes that of man]–blessed (happy, fortunate, and enviable) is he." [I Samuel 3:1; Amos 8:11, 12.]*

Proverbs 29:18 AMPC

We see another powerful Redemptive Revelation in the book of Revelation, chapter 21:10-13.

*"And he carried me away in the Spirit to a great and high mountain, and showed me the great city, the holy Jerusalem, descending out of heaven from God, having the glory of God. Her light was like a most precious stone, like a jasper stone, clear as crystal. Also, she had a great and high wall with twelve gates, and twelve angels at **the gates, and names written on them, which are the names of the twelve tribes of the children of Israel**: three gates on the east, three gates on the north, three gates on the south, and three gates on the west."*

Do you know what those 12 names on those 12 gates communicate to us today? They tell us God's not afraid of or intimidated by family drama and dysfunction! None of it will stop God's love and redemptive plan in your life if you will just keep your eyes on King Jesus. The Bible is not a Facebook post with all the perfect moments in life captured and shared. It's also not a rant on all the things that are wrong in the world. God is not a social justice warrior. He is the Author and Giver of all life. **He is a Father who did not and does not give up on His family.**

When you read through the book of Genesis you find all kinds of family drama and toxic behavior. You'll find things like: dysfunction, co-dependence, frustration, anger, revenge, corruption, betrayal, deception and lying, stealing, jealousy, envy, rejection, fornication, manipulation, hatred, attempted murder, neglect, disappointment, rape, depression, abuse, confusion, conspiracy, and favoritism! **And that's just to name a few!** Yet God's redemptive love and power has those 12 men's names on the eternal city gates of the heavenly New Jerusalem. Abraham's great grandchildren are eternally honored and remembered.

Will you let God write your redemption story? Your story before and after Christ will be a powerful testimony to the world that God is fighting for you! Remember, don't let things matter more if they don't matter most! If life has touched you wrong, then never forget the love of God in Christ has touched you right. Which is going to matter more?

When it comes to the Mission of Love or the Great Commission, the greatest example we have is Jesus! Let's see Him in action in John chapter 4 on one of His travel days. In John Chapter 4 there is an example of how the Great Commission can be walked out in everyday life. Here Jesus ministers to a woman at a well outside a city of Samaria. As He begins a conversation with her, she brings up racial tension and prejudice between the Jews and the Samaritans. **Jesus did not let what she didn't see change what He did see.** He loved her and therefore had a word of knowledge which took the conversation in a whole new direction. Praise God you and I have all the graces mentioned in I Corinthians 12 available to us today as well.

Now the conversation is about spiritual realities and dealing with spiritual questions that were in her heart all the time. Remember, the Bible says God has put a sense of eternity in every heart (Ecclesiastes 3:11). If you simply love people, God will equip you to connect with people on a truly spiritual and eternal level. This does not guarantee they will open up and receive, but it will give them the opportunity to be reconciled to God.

There are so many ways to open up a person's heart. One of the greatest keys is asking questions! It's fascinating to look through the Gospel accounts and see all the questions Jesus asked. He sometimes even answered questions with questions. Jesus said something very interesting to this woman and I believe it's key to understanding and ministering the Gospel to people. It's a key to help them see **the place** He has prepared for them.

Jesus said to the woman in John 4, if she drank the water He offered, then she would **never thirst again.** People are thirsty! That's a key piece of knowledge. We must understand that people are thirsty. Many times, they don't know they are thirsty. Thirst can be expressed in many different ways. Thirst can be seen as anger, offense, jealousy, fear, addiction, frustration, pride, confusion, insecurity, bullying, anxiety, low self-esteem, and any number of other negative attributes.

Once a person really drinks of Jesus' love and of the Gospel, they are able to live life **never thirsting again!** Once they let Jesus tell them who they really are they will never be in need again! They will be IN CHRIST! When we live in Christ, no one ever needs to appreciate us, recognize us, or treat us right for us to be healthy, whole, and strong. We truly have A WELL OF LIFE springing up into everlasting life. Wow! Nothing is able to separate us from the love of God which is in Christ Jesus (Romans 8:38,39). If we can't be separated from His love, then how can we ever be in need of love again?

If you cannot be separated from love, then you can't be separated from the wisdom and direction you need. If you can't be separated from love, then you can't be separated from the healing or provision you need. If you can't be separated from love, then you can't be separated from the encouragement and hope you need. If you can't be separated from love, then you cannot be made to thirst, which takes the enemy's ability to entice you away. It doesn't mean temptation doesn't come: Jesus was tempted. It does mean that the pull of temptation gets less, and less, and less. In fact, temptation had so little pull-on Jesus that He had to be led by the Spirit into the wilderness and be told to fast 40 days before the tempter could even get an audience with Him. The rest of the time Jesus paid him no mind at all. When you submit to God you are resisting the devil. It's not a two-step process. Just one step, submit to God. God who is Love! God who is Light! In the light you become love through the new birth and the work of the Holy Spirit. You are totally reset to man's original perspective before sin entered with its cronies: shame, guilt, and condemnation.

This place of being seated with Jesus can affect your life every single day! You live with the same eye and perspective He had when He walked the earth. If you don't see Jesus saying it or thinking it, then you cannot allow it or make excuses for it in your life. For instance, if He never got an attitude and felt sorry for Himself, neither should we. If He never worried and got His heart broken, then neither should we.

People will many times say, "God gave me my emotions!" Or "God gave me my feelings!" Yes, but that needs to be illuminated by the counsel of the Word of God. Actually, God didn't give the emotions and feelings we grew up with. Adam gave us those feelings and emotions. We were born of Adam, with his fallen nature, emotions, and feelings, therefore we all have sinned! This means all our feelings and emotions have been self-centered and selfish from birth. **This is why we must be born-again.**

Too many times we're studying the fallen man to figure out who we are. You're to study the Heavenly Man to figure out who you really are. Jesus is the Heavenly Man, and you're destined to be conformed to His image (I Corinthians 15:49). In fact, Romans 8:19-22 says the world is groaning in travail waiting for the manifestation of the sons of God. It's time for the world to see a true son of God. This includes all you ladies, too! The world needs to see a child of God who's no longer thirsty and drinking from the wells of this world, but full of joy that comes from the well of salvation inside of them - the fullness of Love that is in them!

It's time for the world to see a Christian who doesn't let sin against them produce sin in them. It's time for Christians to not let what people don't see and understand change what they do see and understand.

Like it says in II Corinthians 5:16, it's time to no longer know people according to the flesh, but according to the spirit- that's according to Love! When it comes to the Great Commission or the Mission of Love, you can learn a whole lot from the life of Joseph. Again, like Isaac, his life is a perfect example of Jesus. Let's take a minute and talk about Joseph's bones. That's right, Joseph's bones. Joseph gave instructions concerning his bones when the children of Israel came out of Egypt. He asked his people to take his bones with them when God visits them (Genesis 50:24,25). Was Joseph just being weird? Why would did he request this?

There may be other answers to this, but what the Lord has revealed to me is this: what was in his bones would need to be in their bones in order to follow God all the way into the promised land. In other words, the perspective of his life would be the perspective they would need. The lessons he learned would need to instruct them. The first generation which failed to get in obviously didn't learn the lessons that Joseph's life teaches us. **Life is not**

about our comfort and our surviving; it's about His perspective and His eternal purposes, all of which is the Mission of Love!

I want you to listen closely to the Holy Spirit as you look with me at the verses where Joseph reveals himself to his brothers - his brothers who had put him in the pit and sold him into slavery, all because of their envy and jealousy. They had even written him off concerning family and lied to their father about Joseph's death. I especially want you to notice how he seeks to comfort them and seeks to help them understand a perspective he had discovered through his faith and trust in God!

> *"Then he said: 'I am Joseph your brother, whom you sold into Egypt. **But now, do not therefore be grieved or angry with yourselves because you sold me here; for God sent me before you to preserve life.** For these two years the famine has been in the land, and there are still five years in which there will be neither plowing nor harvesting. And God sent me before you to preserve a posterity for you in the earth, and to save your lives by a great deliverance. So now it was not you who sent me here, but God; and He has made me a father to Pharaoh, and lord*

*of all his house, and a ruler throughout all the
land of Egypt.'"*

Genesis 45:4–8

It's so important to notice in Genesis 45:5 where Joseph is trying to comfort them when they realize their sin is exposed and Joseph is in a place of absolute power to be both judge and jury. The way he speaks to them sounds a lot like Jesus on the cross saying, "Father forgive them for they know not what they do" (Luke 23:34). Sounds a whole lot like Stephen, whom Saul put to death, saying, "Lord, do not charge them with this sin" (Acts 7:60).

When the Gospel cuts the heart, **and it should,** you must immediately help others to see the Mission of Love. This is what Peter did in Acts 2:37-39 after preaching. We also must help others to see they have been saved by Love and they have been saved to Love! They are no longer in need of love; having been born-again they are love.

Saved by Love
Saved to Love

Now back to Joseph and his brothers. Let's fast forward several years, after their father died, and I want you to see how hard forgiveness can be to receive!

*"When Joseph's brothers saw that their father was dead, they said, 'Perhaps Joseph will hate us, and may actually repay us for all the evil which we did to him.' So, they sent messengers to Joseph, saying, 'Before your father died, he commanded, saying, "Thus you shall say to Joseph: 'I beg you, please forgive the trespass of your brothers and their sin; for they did evil to you.'"' Now, please, forgive the trespass of the servants of the God of your father.' And Joseph wept when they spoke to him. Then his brothers also went and fell down before his face, and they said, 'Behold, we are your servants.' Joseph said to them 'Do not be afraid, for am I in the place of God? But as for you, you meant evil against me; but God meant it for good, in order to bring it about as it is this day, to save many people alive. **Now therefore, do not be afraid; I will provide for you and your little ones.' And he comforted them and spoke kindly to them."***

Genesis 50:15-21

These brothers have already been forgiven and comforted and provided for by Joseph for many years. He had kept his every word to them while maintaining a compassionate and merciful heart towards them. Yet when their father died, they thought surely Joseph would seize his opportunity to repay them. **Notice how hard it can be to believe and receive absolute grace and mercy.** I've heard it said by some that the Gospel could be called the too good to be true news! I know that's a man's spin on things, but it really is a struggle for some to receive absolute grace and mercy.

Consequently, it then becomes hard to show others absolute grace and mercy: a Divine Reset! This is why Colossians 1:7 in the Passion Translation calls the Gospel **"an astonishing revelation!"** The other side of this coin is that many times you may not have truly forgiven others, even though you say, "Oh, I forgive them." Here are some bullet points of what the absolute grace and forgiveness of Joseph looks like. This is exactly what the absolute forgiveness of Jesus looks like as well. I give you these first of all, to make sure you receive them fully, but also to make sure you demonstrate them fully.

Some people will never darken the doors of a church building, no matter how comfortable or relevant we make our services. The only chance they have to be touched by the love of God is to experience it in the life of a Christian. They must encounter an Ambassador of Christ. They must encounter a Minister of Reconciliation. They must encounter a Child of God.

From the life of Joseph, here's what we can learn about dealing with our adversaries:

Genesis 37:5-11 ....45:1-8 ... 50:15-21

- You do not tell anyone what someone did to you. You're not seeking to spread it and you do not want to injure their reputation, rather you want to protect them and their reputation.

- You won't let anyone be afraid of you. You don't want them intimidated or even uncomfortable in your presence.

- You won't want them to continue feeling guilty.

- You let them save face.

- You keep from the world their darkest secret. Remember, love covers a multitude of sins, and it covered yours. Consider the sons of Noah in this matter. **Covering it does not mean you're excusing it.**

- You realize forgiveness is a lifelong commitment. Jesus said in Luke 17 to forgive 7x70 times regarding just one person who sins against you in a day. That's an inexhaustible amount of mercy.

- You bless them and want to see them blessed. You use your power and influence to increase them and not diminish them. This will many times be expressed in prayer for them!

I encourage you to take the time to read the above portions of scripture and see that these points are simply lifted right out of the scriptures! These points first relate to how we receive the absolute forgiveness of God. Then they help us to express the absolute forgiveness of God. Even if you struggle to receive or give this quality of forgiveness, get alone with the Lord, and thank Him for forgiving you this way. Thank Him that His love has been poured out in your heart by the Holy Spirit and you are totally capable of being loved and loving like He loves! Meditate on these truths and spend time in His presence until you experience what Jesus said, "Learn of Me for I am meek and lowly of heart and My yoke is easy and My burden is light!" (Matthew 11:29,30)

For me it's hard to talk about the Mission of Love and not talk about the Moravians. God used the Moravian Prayer and Missionary movement to speak to us as a family. During our years working in Europe on the mission field we prayed much in line with what had been prayed by the Moravians.

"Our Lamb Has Overcome, Let us follow Him!"

The words quoted above come from the Moravian believers of the 1700's and early 1800's. During a 100+ year prayer watch that was 24 hours a day, over 300 missionaries were sent out into the world. The first two men that began this missionary movement actually sold themselves into slavery to reach the slaves of the West Indies. As the ship departed and as loved ones said their final goodbyes, these two men were heard to have cried out what became the holy cry of the Moravian believers.

"May the Lamb receive the reward of His suffering!"

They later had a flag made with the words I quoted above, "Our Lamb has overcome, let us follow Him!" Jesus told us to take up our cross and follow Him. I trust by reading this book you can clearly see **the place** we have with God and the purpose we have with God. **Let's take up the Mission of Love and follow Him! After all, it's impossible to love the Savior of men and not love the men that He saved!**

Here are some critical Mission Points to meditate on as a Soldier of the Cross!

Abide in His love and be with Him in His presence.

Do not let sin against you excuse or produce sin in you.

Always worship from a place of intimacy, agreement, and partnership with Him! Trust and obey with JOY His every instruction.

Do not let what people don't see and understand change what you do see and understand.

Always welcome the conviction of the Holy Spirit. Repent while refusing the voice of shame, guilt, and condemnation. (I John 1:9) Simply return to the top!

Do not let something matter more if it doesn't matter most.

Realize there are no more bad days, only opportunities to shine. (Isaiah 60:1-3)

Do not live life in need of love. Live life as an expression of love. You're a city on a hill which cannot be hidden. (Matthew 5:14)

"Let us consider one another in order to stir up love

and good works, not forsaking the assembling together, as is the manner of some, but exhort one another, and so much the more as we see the Day approaching." (Hebrews 10: 24,25)

Every day Love wakes you up. Every day you're a minister and have a ministry. You're a Minister of Reconciliation with a Word of Reconciliation. You're an Ambassador for Christ. Let your home become your Mission Base and your daily work become an expression of worship. (II Corinthians 5:17-21)

Never forget the cross is where God's perfect justice and mercy came together. Love has given us the Gospel. It has the dual power to cut and to heal the hearts of men. Love has given you a Gospel that engrafted you into Christ so that the same life that's in Him could flow in you!

I would like to encourage you to take some pictures along the way. As the opportunities come to love people and touch them with the power and love of Christ: honor and celebrate the moment with them with a picture. It's important to honor and remember Love's victories. Then if you want, post them to Facebook and social media with the #FamilyMission, #DivineReset, and #TruthThatTransforms.

As we do this, we can encourage, inspire, and challenge one another in the Family Mission. Together we can revive the Mission of Love! Together we can make every home a Mission Base! Together we will become a fellowship of Missionaries!

**Soldiers of Compassion.
Soldiers of the Cross.**

A Glorious Church

Throughout this book I've talked about the importance of keeping scriptures in context. Letting the Bible interpret the Bible. There's a reason for that. You could surgically patch scriptures together and make the Bible say just about whatever you wanted it to say. We've all probably done it in some form or fashion. Had a belief first and then tried to find support for that belief in the Bible, rather than letting the Bible tell us what to believe. What to believe about God. What to believe about ourselves. What to believe about our circumstances. What to believe about our situations.

Early in my walk with the Lord, I was shown a passage in the Scripture from a man who was discipling and mentoring me. This passage marked my life and put into motion a discipline that blesses and strengthens my walk with the Lord to this very day. I want to share it with you now.

It's found in Deuteronomy 17. These were God's instructions to the kings who would rule over the nation of Israel.

*"When you come to the land which the Lord your God is giving you, and possess it and dwell in it, and say, 'I will set a king over me like all the nations that are around me,' you shall surely set a king over you whom the Lord your God chooses; one from among your brethren you shall set as king over you; you may not set a foreigner over you, who is not your brother. But he shall not multiply horses for himself, nor cause the people to return to Egypt to multiply horses, for the Lord has said to you, 'You shall not return that way again.' Neither shall he multiply wives for himself, lest his heart turn away; nor shall he greatly multiply silver and gold for himself. "Also it shall be, when he sits on the throne of his kingdom, that **he shall write for himself a copy of this law in a book, from the one before the priests, the Levites.** And it shall be with him, and he shall read it all the days of his life, **that he may learn to fear the Lord his God** and be careful to observe all the words of this law and these statutes, **that his heart may not be lifted above***

> *his brethren, that he may not turn aside from the commandment to the right hand or to the left, and that he may prolong his days in his kingdom, he and his children in the midst of Israel."*

Deuteronomy 17:14-20

You might be saying, what is the point, Mark? First of all, the Bible is speaking to the King in you. If every seed produces after its kind and King Jesus planted His life, then what kind of harvest is He expecting? If corn produces corn and beans produce beans, then kings would produce kings! Christ in you, the hope of glory means there's a king in you. If you're born-again by the royal blood of Jesus, then you are now a part of the royal Family of God. Remember, mankind is still under a dominion mandate from Genesis 1. Having dominion is clearly language that would be spoken to kings. Jesus is called the King of kings and the Lord of lords. Look at this passage in Revelation chapter 1 in case there's any doubt left.

"From Jesus Christ, the faithful witness, the firstborn from the dead, and the ruler over the kings of the earth. To Him who loved us and washed us from our sins in His own blood and has made us kings and priests to His God and Father, to Him be glory and dominion forever and ever. Amen."

Here's one more passage in Romans chapter 5 that will further clarify things in our hearts along these lines.

"For if because of one man's trespass (lapse, offense) death reigned through that one, much more surely will those who receive [God's] overflowing grace (unmerited favor) and the free gift of righteousness [putting them into right standing with Himself] **reign as kings in life through the one Man Jesus Christ** *(the Messiah, the Anointed One)."*

Romans 5:17 AMPC

With all these scriptures in clear view regarding God's intent, let's look again at the passage in Deuteronomy 17. Let's see why you need to have such a healthy and thriving relationship with the Word of God.

First, a king was to write for himself a copy of the Word of God he had at that time. He could not hire it done! He was to write a copy for himself. There is something so powerful about writing the Word of God and writing the revelations down that you receive from the Word of God. I encourage you to carefully journal your walk with God through writing down the scriptures and the light that transform your thinking. I do things both electronically and on paper. Please note. Copying and pasting from a Bible app is not the same. There's something about writing or typing that just makes it more personal and intimate.

Next, we see that he was to read it every day of his life. That's right, every day of his life. Every day of his life he was to read the Word of God. It is so very important that you read it out loud whenever possible. Faith comes by hearing and hearing by the Word of God. No better voice than your own to nourish your faith in God. Your relationship with God is greatly influenced by your personal relationship with the inspired scriptures. Please don't let that be too simple. Brother Kenneth E. Hagin used to say all the time, "Many people miss the supernatural because they are always looking for the spectacular." The Bible is a supernatural book. You'll find as you read a question may rise up in your heart. So, the question arises.

Am I reading the Bible or is the Bible reading me?

Your relationship with the Bible will make your life supernaturally blessed and increased. Finally, we see in this passage several results God wanted for His kings. These results come from a thriving healthy relationship with the Word of God. Here is a simple summary:

- That he may learn to fear the Lord his God.

- That he would be careful to observe all the words of the law and the statutes.

- That his heart would not be lifted up in pride above all his brethren.

- That he would not turn aside from the commandment to the right or to the left.

- That he would prolong his days in the kingdom.

- That he and his children would walk in the ways of the Lord his God.

Each of these points could be further explained, but for my purposes here today I will just mention them. This is why you need to learn to honor and greatly respect the scriptures, always keeping them in context and always letting the Bible interpret the Bible. By doing this over the years I have actually had to change some of the things I believed. That's okay. I need to read the Bible to find out what and who to believe, rather than simply reading it to confirm what I already believe. Let's look at a few final passages along these lines before we begin pressing into **a glorious church**, because these are all foundational to what we believe about **a glorious church!**

"THUS SAYS the Lord: Heaven is My throne, and the earth is My footstool. What kind of house would you build for Me? And what kind can be My resting-place? [Acts 17:24.] For all these things My hand has made, and so all these things have come into being [by and for Me], says the Lord. But this is the man to whom I will look and have regard: **he who is humble and of a broken or wounded spirit, and who trembles at My word and reveres My commands.** *[John 4:24.]."*

Isaiah 66:1-2 AMPC

Do you really want God's attention? If you do, He told you right here through His prophet Isaiah how to get it. It's through your humility and your hunger for the Word of God. His Word contains His Voice. The power and purpose of the Word of God is also revealed by the prophet Jeremiah. He said the Word of God will **root out, pull down, destroy, overthrow, build and plant** (Jeremiah 1:9,10).

Paul told Timothy, *"Every Scripture is God-breathed (given by His inspiration) and profitable for* **instruction,** *for* **reproof** *and* **conviction** *of sin, for* **correction** *of error and* **discipline** *in obedience, [and] for* **training** *in righteousness (in holy living, in conformity to God's will in* *thought, purpose, and action), So that the man of God may be complete and proficient, well fitted and **thoroughly equipped** for every good work," (2 Timothy 3:16-17 AMPC).*

The Word of God is for our …

Instruction
Reproof
Conviction
Correction
Discipline
Training
Equipping

The writer of Hebrews said it this way: "*For the Word that God speaks is alive and full of power [making it active, operative, energizing, and effective]; it is sharper than any two-edged sword, penetrating to the dividing line of the breath of life (soul) and [the immortal] spirit, and of joints and marrow [of the deepest parts of our nature], exposing and sifting and analyzing and judging the very thoughts and purposes of the heart. And not a creature exists that is concealed from His sight, but all things are open and exposed, naked, and defenseless to the eyes of Him with Whom we have to do." Hebrews 4:12-13 AMPC*

I have taken time to explain all of this because of its

tremendous importance, but also, so that you can clearly see the context of the phrase ***a glorious church.*** As you read this passage, I want you to let the Bible interpret itself, and therefore let the tree land where it falls! Simply let the truth fall where it lands! Let's now take a look at **a glorious church** in its natural habitat, or as I like to say, in its original context.

*"Submit to one another in the fear of God. Wives, submit to your own husbands, as to the Lord. For the husband is head of the wife, as also Christ is head of the church; and He is the Savior of the body. Therefore, just as the church is subject to Christ, so let the wives be to their own husbands in everything. Husbands, love your wives, just as Christ also loved the church and gave Himself for her, that He might sanctify and cleanse her with the washing of water by the word, that He might present her to Himself **a glorious church,** not having spot or wrinkle or any such thing, but that she should be holy and without blemish. So, husbands ought to love their own wives as their own bodies; he who loves his wife loves himself. For no one ever hated his own flesh, but nourishes and cherishes it, just as the Lord does the church.*

For we are members of His body, of His flesh and of His bones. "For this reason a man shall leave his father and mother and be joined to his wife, and the two shall become one flesh." This is a great mystery, but I speak concerning Christ and the church. Nevertheless, let each one of you in particular so love his own wife as himself, and let the wife see that she respects her husband."

Ephesians 5:21-33

The **Holy Spirit intentionally** put this phrase in the context of His instructions to family, especially in His instructions to marriage, and mainly in His instructions to men! Why are marriage and family under such attack from the enemy? Why? **Because covenant family is the eternal framework upon which we will rule and reign with King Jesus throughout the ages.**

Like I said in chapter three on True Worshippers, worship according to Genesis 22 is a covenant family working together in covenant love fulfilling a Kingdom covenant purpose. No wonder marriage and family are under such assault and are so confused in our day and age. No wonder the enemy has worked to bring such pain and suffering into the home.

The Lord released a powerful prophetic word through us years ago. He said, **"If you heal the home, you can heal the land."** Praise God! That's why Family Mission exists, to bring healing to the home. This is why this book is in your hands- to bring healing to your home. I mentioned earlier about the seven mountains or territories of influence in culture today. If all of these mountains or territories are going to be influenced by the Kingdom of God, then you need to bring healing to the home. No matter where someone works and no matter what gifts and graces are in their lives, at the end of the day, they are going home. If the home has not been healed, then there are going to be limitations on how effective a person will be elsewhere in life.

According to the passage above marriage itself is given a mandate by Scripture. *"For we are members of His body, of His flesh and of His bones. For this reason, a man shall leave his father and mother and be joined to his wife, and the two shall become one flesh. This is a great mystery, but I speak concerning Christ and the church."*

The covenant of marriage is the seed of a family. The covenant you have with Christ is the seed of the reborn family of God. The first Adam had a family tree from which we all had our natural birth. The last Adam planted a new family tree from which we can all have a spiritual new birth. This is why Jesus said you must be born-again (John 3:3). Scripture calls us the bride of Christ. Being a bride in these terms is not a gender issue. This is all about your covenant relationship with Christ. Being the bride of Christ means you are the covenant partner of Christ throughout all of eternity.

Never forget He found you and He chose you. He pursued you. He proposed to you on the cross! Now it's up to every soul on the planet to decide, will they say YES? Maybe you've never thought of it exactly that way, but the cross was and is a proposal. Christ is saying, "I know you. I know all that you've done. **However, I also know things about you from the beginning.** Therefore, I want you. I choose you. Will you join me in covenant love?" So, as we read through this passage in Ephesians 5 and see the Holy Spirit's instructions to marriage and family, you can see how all of this lives out eternally through the family of God, through **a glorious church!**

I'm going to make a bold statement that I want you to consider. It is scripturally unreasonable to expect a **glorious church** to rise up without making marriage and family everything God intended from the beginning.   There has to be a Divine Reset! Yes, we need to pray for **a glorious church,** but we need to embrace the reality of this context chosen by the Holy Spirit. You need to let the Bible interpret the Bible. The letter of the Ephesians is exactly that, it's a letter.

We have chapter and verse for reference's sake, but they were written as letters. It's always healthy to read the epistles from time to time in their entirety. This way you catch the flow of the scriptures. Therefore chapter 6 of Ephesians is vitally connected to chapter 5. Here's what it says in the first few verses of chapter 6.

"Children, obey your parents in the Lord, for this is right. "Honor your father and mother," which is the first commandment with promise: "that it may be well with you and you may live long on the earth." And you, fathers, do not provoke your children to wrath, but bring them up in the training and admonition of the Lord. Bondservants, be obedient to those who are your masters according to the flesh, with fear and trembling, in sincerity of heart, as to Christ; not with eye-service, as men-pleasers, but as bondservants of Christ, doing the will of God from the heart, with goodwill doing service, as to the Lord, and not to men, knowing that whatever good anyone does, he will receive the same from the Lord, whether he is a

slave or free. And you, masters, do the same things to them, giving up threatening, knowing that your own Master also is in heaven, and there is no partiality with Him."

Ephesians 6:1-9

Do you see the connection? He just finished speaking to wives and husbands. He just spoke of **a glorious church** as he gave instructions to husbands. Now he's going to give instructions to children and then on to employees and employers! That pretty much relationally sums up all of our lives, doesn't it? Everyone is born into the earth because of the intimacy between a man and a woman, whether they're married or not. Everyone is a child of a mom and dad somewhere, whether you know them or not, whether you like them or not, whether they raised you or not. Also, everyone is to be working and producing. God even gave man work in the Garden of Eden. God is a producer and man is to be a producer. God works and man is to work with God.

I think it's important to use the word *work* rather than the word *job*. Not that *job* is a wrong word or a bad word, but many times a job is just tied to a paycheck. You were never intended to work for a paycheck. You were given work to create and produce. You were given work to partner with God. You were given work to express the God given graces in your life. You were given work to replenish the earth with the Kingdom of God. There is certainly a lot of work that needs to be done!

The good news of Jesus Christ is for all tribes, all tongues, all peoples, and all nations! Notice the Bible doesn't use the word race! I want to say that again. The Bible doesn't use the word race. I know certain translations do, but in the original language it's not there. That's a word man and certain translators have chosen to use. Race is the root of racism! The Bible uses the words tribe, tongues, peoples, and nations.

Here are some incredible passages along these lines.

> *"And they sang a new song, saying: ‹You are worthy to take the scroll, And to open its seals; For You were slain, And have redeemed us to God by Your blood Out of every tribe and tongue and people and nation, '"*

Revelation 5:9

> *"After these things I looked, and behold, a great multitude which no one could number, of all nations, tribes, peoples, and tongues, standing before the throne and before the Lamb, clothed with white robes, with palm branches in their hands, "*

Revelation 7:9

"Then those from the peoples, tribes, tongues, and nations will see their dead bodies three-and-a-half days, and not allow their dead bodies to be put into graves."

Revelation 11:9

"Then I saw another angel flying in the midst of heaven, having the everlasting Gospel to preach to those who dwell on the earth—to every nation, tribe, tongue, and people—"

Revelation 14:6

A glorious church will consist of all nations, all tribes, all tongues, and all peoples. Glory to God forever and ever amen! Family is a structure that exists all around the world. Family is a structure that will exist throughout all eternity. If we're going to see **a glorious church** rise up and emerge in our generation then we need to hang all the truths of the Bible on the framework of family and not manmade religious systems!

In 1994 when we established Living Waters Fellowship, the Lord Jesus said to us, "You're NOT starting a church, I already did that." He told us, "You're starting a fellowship within THE church. I started the church in the book of Acts and I'm still building it this very day." He also spoke these words to us through our pastor, "A strong church is made of strong families, because THE church is a family!"

One of the most important things we were directed to do from the very beginning was to apply the blood of Jesus over our marriage and family and over the fellowship that we planted and pastored, just like Moses was instructed to do over the homes and houses of the Israelites. These instructions were found in Exodus chapter 12.

> *"Then Moses called for all the elders of Israel and said to them, "Pick out and take lambs for yourselves according to your families, and kill the Passover lamb. And you shall take a bunch of hyssops, dip it in the blood that is in the basin, and* **strike the lintel and the two doorposts with the blood that is in the basin**. *And none of you shall go out of the door of his house until morning. "*

Exodus 12:21-22

Israel had to do this with real blood and a branch of hyssop, but today you can also apply the blood of Jesus in your life, family, and home. You do it in faith and with your words. You use the hyssop of your tongue I like to say. Here are a few revelations and declarations that we have used for decades in our lives. I believe it's one of the main reasons the Lord has protected and blessed our life and family so very much. For decades, my wife and I have declared these truths nearly daily.

Revelations and Declarations of the Blood of Jesus to be spoken out loud and in faith!

The blood of Jesus cleanses me from all defilement of the enemy.

The blood of Jesus prevents deceptions and aborts every attempt of the enemy to deceive me.

The blood of Jesus reconciles everything in me to the perfect will of God every day and in every way.

The blood of Jesus is my divine covering and protection. Angels are active in my life because of the blood of Jesus.

The blood of Jesus produces a righteousness consciousness in me.

The blood of Jesus seeded the divine nature of agape love in me. I now have a type A personality. Type Agape!

I have a new D N A ... I have the **Divine Nature of Agape.**

Your words over your life, family, and home are extremely influential. The scripture says in the book of Proverbs, *"Through skillful and godly Wisdom is a house **(a life, a home, a family)** built, and by understanding it is established [on a sound and good foundation], And by knowledge shall its chambers [of every area] be filled with all precious and pleasant riches"* Proverbs 24:3-4 AMPC.

Through faith and the application of the blood of Jesus you will release supernatural wisdom, understanding and knowledge from the Word of God in your life. Words are powerful. According to Proverbs 18:21 they either contain life or they contain death. **No words are just empty.** I want to say that again. **No words are just empty.** This is why Jesus said you would have to give an account for every word that you would speak.

"But I tell you, on the day of judgment men will have to give account for every idle (inoperative, nonworking) word they speak. ***For by your words, you will be justified and acquitted, and by your words you will be condemned and sentenced."***

Matthew 12:36-37 AMPC

Spoken words were how THE BLESSING was placed upon lives, homes, and families throughout the Bible.

Blessing that would flow from generation to generation to generation. We pray you will begin releasing it on your house, home, and family by faith with the hyssop of your words, **using your voice!**

This is especially important for Fathers and Dads!

In many ways **you are the most important prophetic voice in your life.** Why? It's the power of speaking blessing, speaking life, speaking truth by declaring the end from the beginning! Even if a prophet speaks a word over your life, it only becomes a reality and is fulfilled when it is upon your lips! When it's released in agreement and faith with your words.

Again, I am convinced this is a major reason my life, marriage and sons have been so very blessed and protected. These very principles go all the way back to the early days of God's covenant family: Abraham, Isaac, and Jacob (Israel). God is a generational God. Until you think generationally you will never partner with God like He desires.

I want to share with you an interesting part of the story of Jacob (Israel). In this story Jacob (Israel) and his mother Rebekah conspired to steal **the blessing.** It's an interesting story that can teach us a lot. Esau, the oldest, was supposed to receive the firstborn blessing but Jacob took that blessing away from him. That's right, he took it! Think about it!

Jacob essentially stole spoken words!

This might have been the first identity theft ever recorded. Here's the account of it found in Genesis 27:5-10:

"Now Rebekah was listening when Isaac spoke to Esau his son. And Esau went to the field to hunt game and to bring it. So, Rebekah spoke to Jacob her son, saying, 'Indeed I heard your father speak to Esau your brother, saying, «Bring me game and make savory food for me, that I may eat it and bless you in the presence of the Lord before my death.» Now therefore, my son, obey my voice according to what I command you. Go now to the flock and bring me from there two choice kids of the goats, and I will make savory food from them for your father, such as he loves. Then you shall take it to your father, that he may eat it, and that he may bless you before his death.'"

The blessing was from God, but it was released through Isaac's faith filled spoken words over Jacob (Israel). The Bible references this very account in Hebrews chapter 11. Many have called this chapter in Hebrews God's Hall of Fame of Faith. It's filled with great men and women who are commonly called our heroes of Faith.

*"[With eyes of] faith Isaac, looking far into the future, invoked (**by speaking**) blessings upon Jacob and Esau. [Gen. 27:27-29, 39, 40.]".*

Hebrews 11:20 AMPC

Remember there are no empty words.

"Death and life are in the power of the tongue, and they who indulge in it shall eat the fruit of it [for death or life]. [Matt. 12:37.]."

Proverbs 18:21 AMPC

Jacob, who became Israel, eventually did the same thing with the sons of Joseph.

"[Prompted] by faith Jacob, when he was dying, blessed each of Joseph's sons and bowed in prayer over the top of his staff. [Gen. 48.]"

Hebrews 11:21 AMPC

It is essential that we take a look at another important way to apply the blood of Jesus to your life, home, and family.

**Another important way you apply
the blood of Jesus to your life
is to be vitally connected to
His body, the body of Christ!**

It's impossible to get blood flow if you're disconnected from the body of Christ. Yes, you are by faith in relationship with Him, but you are also by faith in relationship with His body. You can't just love the head and not love the body.

How many wives would like their husbands to love their head only and give no attention or respect to their body? Or vice versa for the men? That would be weird, wouldn't it? Yet many Christians claim to love Jesus, but simply will not commit to a vital relationship with His body! Paul, who wrote about **a glorious church** to the Ephesians, also wrote to the Corinthians about the body of Christ.

> *"For as the body is one and has many members, but **all the members of that one body, being many, are one body, so also is Christ.** For by one Spirit, we were all baptized into one body—whether Jews or Greeks, whether slaves or free—and have all been made to drink into one Spirit. **For in fact the body is not one***

member but many. *But now indeed there are many members, yet one body. And the eye cannot say to the hand, "I have no need of you;" nor again the head to the feet, "I have no need of you." No, much rather, those members of the body which seem to be weaker are necessary. And those members of the body which we think to be less honorable, on these we bestow greater honor; and our unpresentable parts have greater modesty, but our presentable parts have no need.* **But God composed the body, having given greater honor to that part which lacks it, that there should be no schism in the body, but that the members should have the same care for one another. Now you are the body of Christ, and members individually."**

I Corinthians 12:12-14, 20-25, 27

A glorious church is seen as a glorious body.

A glorious church is seen as a glorious family.

A glorious church is seen as a glorious home.

A glorious church is seen as a glorious marriage.

A glorious church is seen as a glorious covenant relationship.

In I John 1:3,4 you have a beautiful description of the relationship between an individual's faith and the faith that you share in a fellowship family.

*"That which we have seen and heard we declare to you, **that you also may have fellowship with us;** and truly **our fellowship is with the Father and with His Son Jesus Christ.** And these things we write to you **that your joy may be full."***

One of the ways you can share the Gospel is when you share your testimony. Psalm 107:2 NIV says, *"Let the redeemed of the Lord tell their story!"* When you tell your redemption story, when you testify of what you have seen and what you have heard, then you are making an invitation. You are inviting someone to come home in their heart just like you did when you said yes to Jesus, when you believed in your heart and confessed with your mouth that God raised Him from the dead for your justification of sin. (Romans 10:9,10)

There's no greater redemptive story told in scripture than the one Jesus told of the lost son coming home in Luke 15. In fact, Luke 15 is a trilogy of stories Jesus told of things that were lost and then found - a sheep that was lost, a coin that was lost, and finally, a son that was lost.

Many times, people don't completely understand why we use the *lost* terminology. Truth is simple. Aren't you glad for that? Here's the simple truth about all of these items that were lost. None of them were where they belonged. The sheep belongs with the herd and the shepherd. The coin belonged where the woman kept it safe. The son belonged at home with his father and his family!

Many times, we talk about the prodigal or lost son coming home when someone who knew the Lord walks away and comes back. Yes, that can certainly apply. Yes, that's a beautiful and powerful thing. However, the most powerful application is always in context. Always letting the Bible interpret the Bible.

Since mankind has sinned and fallen short of the glory of God, then all of mankind has wasted its inheritance. We all inherited our life! We all inherited a free will and a free choice, and we all wasted it on ourselves. We all wasted our sovereign free will to do whatever we want. Please take a look at this passage in Galatians 5 in the Message paraphrase.

> *"It is absolutely clear that God has called you to a free life. Just make sure that you don't use this freedom as an excuse to do whatever you*

want to do and destroy your freedom. Rather, use your freedom to serve one another in love; that's how freedom grows. *For everything we know about God's Word is summed up in a single sentence: Love others as you love yourself. That's an act of true freedom. If you bite and ravage each other, watch out—in no time at all you will be annihilating each other, and where will your precious freedom be then?"*

Galatians 5:13-15 MSG.

We all used our freedom as an excuse to do whatever we wanted and ended up destroying our freedom. We all ended up biting, ravaging, and annihilating each other. Now after thousands of years of this we see the world in a corrupt and twisted place. Paul described it to Timothy this way in II Timothy chapter 3:

"But know this, that in the last days perilous times will come: For men will be lovers of themselves, lovers of money, boasters, proud, blasphemers, disobedient to parents, unthankful, unholy, unloving, unforgiving, slanderers, without self-control, brutal, despisers of good, traitors, headstrong, haughty, lovers of pleasure rather

than lovers of God, having a form of godliness but denying its power. And from such people turn away! ... always learning and never able to come to the knowledge of the truth."

II Timothy 3:1-7

A glorious church is a glorious home and a glorious family. You are called by God to be prepared to welcome home lost sons and daughters through the Gospel of Jesus Christ. In all of our homes and fellowships, we need to have our Father's heart!

Like the father of the prodigal son of old, you need to always be looking on the horizon. You need to always be looking for opportunities to welcome a lost son or daughter home. Remember, this is why they are lost. They are not where they belong! They belong with the Father and His family. Remember I John 1:3?

"That which we have seen and heard we declare to you, that you also may have fellowship with us; and truly our fellowship is with the Father and with His Son Jesus Christ."

Jesus said, *"I am the Door!"* You and I get to hold the Door open and always be ready to welcome them home!

What else happened when that son came home? The father celebrated by killing a fattened calf. Sadly, this celebration was not shared by an elder brother who despised his younger brother for running off and wasting the father's inheritance. He claimed to have been a perfect son and accused his father of never celebrating him. Obviously, he was falsely accusing his father.

Yet how many people today are falsely accusing God? They will be the same ones who will have a hard time when lost sons and daughters come home. The father replied with words that will rock your world if you let them. He said, "What my son? Why do you say these things?

ALL THAT I HAVE IS YOURS!"

Wow. That will shake you to the core when you realize that He wants you to know that **all that He has is yours!**

What else did this father do? He put the best robe on him. He put a ring back on his finger and He put sandals back on his feet. Let's talk a little about that. A robe, a ring, and sandals. What do they all represent? When you come home in your heart to the Father, then you have your value, identity, and purpose restored to you as well.

The Father celebrated your return in advance by faith by giving His only begotten Son as a sacrifice. Remember, Jesus said, "No one comes to the Father except through Me." Being **found** or being **saved** has never been about where you go when you die. It's always been about coming home in your heart to your Father and your family. We are all lost and not where we belong! Before we accept Christ, we are already "dead in our trespasses and sins." We need to identify with Him in His death, so that we can identify with Him in our resurrection with Him!

> *'But God, who is rich in mercy, because of His great love with which He loved us, even when we were dead in trespasses, made us alive together with Christ (by grace you have been saved), and raised us up together, and made us sit together in the heavenly places in Christ Jesus, that in the ages to come He might show the exceeding riches of His grace in His kindness toward us in Christ Jesus. For by grace, you have been saved through faith, and that not of yourselves; it is the gift of God,"*

Ephesians 2:4-8

When you come home you get a robe of righteousness to put on. You get a ring of family authority to wear, and you get shoes of divine eternal purpose to wear every day. **A glorious church** will prepare to receive lost sons and daughters home, teaching them how to walk in the righteousness of Jesus Christ and how to reign in life as kings and priests unto God our Father. **A glorious church** will teach them about their authority and dominion that's been restored by being joint heirs with Jesus Christ. **A glorious church** will teach them about everyday purpose and the Mission of Love. A mission that is to be lived out at home and at work.

Every tribe, tongue, people, and nation deserve a chance to come home in their hearts to our Father in Heaven. They all deserve a chance to experience a Divine Reset and embrace their God given destiny as a part of His legacy.

A Glorious Church is a glorious eternal royal covenant family.

The nation of Israel was the family of Abraham in natural terms. They are like the sand of the shore in number. The church of the Lord Jesus Christ is the family of Abraham in spiritual terms. We are like the stars of Heaven in number. Scripture is abundantly clear why God chose Abraham. God chose him because He knew Abraham would keep His walk with God about family and about generational blessing and the legacy of faith in God.

Genesis 18:19 says, *"For I have known him, **in order that he may command his children and his household after him**, that they keep the way of the Lord, to do righteousness and justice, **that the Lord may bring to Abraham what He has spoken to him.**"*

A glorious church is a glorious house. It's the household of faith according to Galatians 6. A glorious church is a place where lost souls are welcomed home. A place where they are welcomed into an eternal royal family. A glorious church is a place where we keep the way of the Lord, and we do righteousness and justice. Why? So, that the Lord may bring upon us all that He has spoken to us!

Let's close out this chapter seeing some of the most profound truths for faith in the blood of Jesus. These truths applied will bring forth **a glorious church, a glorious body, and a glorious bride!** We are going to look now at the seven places Jesus shed His blood. I call these seven facets of the diamond of redemption. These are the seven areas whereby He accomplished a full redemption of ALL THAT WAS LOST!

1. He shed His blood as He sweat blood in the Garden of Gethsemane. As He submitted and surrendered to the Father's wisdom and will, saying, "Nevertheless, not My will but Your will be done!" Remember, it was trust that was lost in the Garden of Eden and our full redemption is beginning with bloodshed in His sweat over TRUSTING the Father's will and wisdom! Never forget this. The biggest enemy to the will of God in your life is Your WILL. It's really not even the devil! It's YOUR WILL. You will die a thousand deaths in order to live a life submitted to the will of God instead of your will. Here's a powerful verse along this line:

"So, SINCE Christ suffered in the flesh for us, for you, arm yourselves with the same thought and purpose [patiently to suffer rather than fail to please God]. For whoever has suffered in the flesh [having the mind of Christ] is done with [intentional] sin [has stopped pleasing himself and the world, and pleases God], So that he can no longer spend the rest of his natural life living by [his] human appetites and desires, but [he lives] for what God wills.

I Peter 4:1-2 AMPC

2. He shed His blood as He was dressed up in mockery as a king. They placed a robe on Him and then twisted a crown of thorns together and pounded it into place on His head. A couple of things here: first of all, man's identity was being redeemed. He was a king, but didn't look like a king in their eyes, so they mocked him and spit on him and put that crown on His head.

Where are the biggest wars you fight every day? It's right between the ears! In your mind. In your head. The blood shed here is winning the biggest battles you will ever fight. Battles over identity and battles of the mind and will. Yet there's still another powerful thing being revealed. When Adam was cursed in the garden of Eden, he was told to work and increase by "the sweat of his brow." Yes, you're supposed to work. God gives man work. But you're not to work according to the flesh but according to the Spirit and grace of life. A common quote you might have heard that illustrates this point is this: "When you're doing what you love you'll never work another day in your life!"

"For though we walk (live) in the flesh, we are not carrying on our warfare according to the flesh and using mere human weapons. For the weapons of our warfare are not physical

[weapons of flesh and blood], but they are mighty before God for the overthrow and destruction of strongholds, [Inasmuch as we] refute arguments and theories and reasonings and every proud and lofty thing that sets itself up against the [true] knowledge of God; and we lead every thought and purpose away captive into the obedience of Christ (the Messiah, the Anointed One), Being in readiness to punish every [insubordinate for his] disobedience, when your own submission and obedience [as a church] are fully secured and complete."

II Corinthians 10:3-6 AMPC

3 & 4. He shed His blood as He was beaten and scourged! He was being punished like Proverbs says a fool is to be punished. The fool says in his heart there is no God. The fool does life the way he thinks is right. Proverbs says in two places, *"There is a way that seems right unto a man, but the end thereof is death."* Jesus took the punishment we deserve. Jesus took the penalty of the righteous judgment of sin. The innocent one took the punishment of the guilty ones. Why? Yes, to fulfill our redemption, but also to give us an example.

*"For to this you were called, because Christ also suffered for us, leaving us an example, that you should follow His steps: "Who committed no sin, Nor was deceit found in His mouth"; who, when He was reviled, did not revile in return; when He suffered, He did not threaten, but committed Himself to Him who judges righteously; who Himself bore our sins in His own body on the tree, **that we, having died to sins, might live for righteousness—by whose stripes you were healed.** For you were like sheep going astray but have now returned to the Shepherd and Overseer of your souls."*

I Peter 2:21-25

By whose stripes you were healed! He bled with both outward wounds, but also inward bruising. So, number 3 and 4 are the inward and the outward bleeding. He was wounded for your transgressions and bruised for your iniquities! He bled outwardly. He bled inwardly. This is so that you can be healed and made whole both outwardly (physically), and inwardly (soulishly and spiritually).

5. He shed His blood as His hands were being pierced with those nails. You might have heard it said this way sometime, "It wasn't the nails that held Him on

the cross, it was His love for you and I." That is exactly the truth! Yet what was being redeemed by the blood shed from His hands?

Have you ever touched something that you shouldn't have? Have you ever built something with your own hands that you shouldn't have? Yes, we all have. The blood of Jesus was shed to redeem all that you did in your own strength, in your own wisdom, and with your own hands.

"Unless the Lord builds the house, They labor in vain who build it; Unless the Lord guards the city, The watchman stays awake in vain. It is vain for you to rise up early, To sit up late, To eat the bread of sorrows; For so He gives His beloved sleep."

Psalms 127:1-2

You need to have the blood of Jesus sanctify and redeem all that you have done and all that you do with your hands.

6. The blood of Jesus was shed as His feet were pierced with those nails. Have you ever walked where you shouldn't have? Have you ever misplaced your purpose? Have you ever walked down a road you were never called to walk? Have you ever run from God

and His plan for your life? Like the prodigal of old, have you ever walked away and left your Father's house?

"My son, attend to my words; consent and submit to my sayings. Let them not depart from your sight; keep them in the center of your heart. For they are life to those who find them, healing, and health to all their flesh. Consider well the path of your feet and let all your ways be established and ordered aright. Turn not aside to the right hand or to the left; remove your foot from evil."

Proverbs 4:20-22, 26-27 AMPC.

The blood of Jesus was shed to redeem all the places your feet have taken you.

Finally let's look at number 7 and see the final place that blood was shed in the Passion of the Christ! I want you to see what was redeemed and what place was prepared for you!

7. The blood was shed as His side was pierced and blood and water flowed! It is understood that in the natural they pierced His side because they wanted to make sure that Jesus was dead. So, the Roman soldier pierced His side. When God wanted to create a

covenant partner for the first Adam what did God do?

*"And the Lord God caused a deep sleep to fall on Adam, and he slept; and **He took one of his ribs, and closed up the flesh in its place.** (He opened up his side!) And Adam said: "This is now bone of my bones And flesh of my flesh; She shall be called Woman, Because she was taken out of Man." Therefore, a man shall leave his father and mother and be joined to his wife, and they shall become one flesh. And they were both naked, the man and his wife, and were not ashamed."*

Genesis 2:21, 23-25

What is the great mystery that Paul gave us in Ephesians 5 as he introduced the idea of **a glorious church**?

*"For we are members of His body, of His flesh and of His bones. "For this reason a man shall leave his father and mother and be joined to his wife, and the two shall become one flesh." **This is a great mystery, but I speak concerning Christ and the church."***

Ephesians 5:30-32

As the blood of Jesus was shed from His side, there was a place being opened up in the body of the last Adam for you. A place was being prepared for you to be one with Him. Take a look at this verse in I Corinthians 6 and prepare to be overwhelmed with the wisdom and goodness of God!

*"Do you not know that your bodies are members of Christ? Shall I then take the members of Christ and make them members of a harlot? Certainly not! Or do you not know that he who is joined to a harlot is one body with her? For **'the two,' He says, 'shall become one flesh.' But he who is joined to the Lord is one spirit with Him.** Flee sexual immorality. Every sin that a man does is outside the body, but he who commits sexual immorality sins against his own body. Or do you not know that your body is the temple of the Holy Spirit who is in you, whom you have from God, and you are not your own? For you were bought at a price; therefore, glorify God in your body and in your spirit, which are God's."*

I Corinthians 6:15-20

When Jesus shed His blood through His side being pierced, He was redeeming the covenant relationship and oneness with God. He was preparing a place at his side for the bride of Christ, the body of Christ, a Glorious Church! Living waters flow today as we walk with Him in covenant love. Church, let's let the blood and water flow from His side today!

When you apply the blood of Jesus to your life, your home, and your family, I want you to use the full understanding of the redeeming blood of Jesus. All of us here at Family Mission want to see a glorious church emerge and rise up in our generation. We cannot, however, surgically extract that phrase from the intentional context the Holy Spirit gave it. We also cannot ignore the final place Jesus shed His blood as His side was opened up as the Last Adam. It was there He made a place for you and me. His covenant partner forever. The Bride of Christ. The Body of Christ. **A Glorious Church!**

Working in Prayer

A little over 25 years ago we were in our third year of prison ministry as an outreach of our local fellowship. Every year we had to go in for recurring training to serve in the prison for another year. Each year it was largely getting to know other volunteers and the prison staff that supported the volunteers. We would fill out paperwork and then hear lectures on contraband in the prison. We would be taught not to share personal information and how not to put yourself in a compromised position relationally with an inmate. From time to time, a specialist would come in and spice it up a bit with some other interesting issues to be prepared for.

This particular year they brought in a specialist who was in charge of handling HOSTAGE situations. That's right, HOSTAGE situations. That got my attention for sure. I knew we were in a prison. I knew we were among maximum security incarcerated criminals, but somehow, I never thought much about being a part of a HOSTAGE situation. Our team was doing a worship service, and everyone was there to worship Jesus right? Or at least learn about Him and His love. Yet, by the end of this presentation, I was thoroughly convinced that it was a realistic threat. Not likely, but a realistic threat none the less.

During this presentation, a statement was made that marked my life forever, and the Holy Spirit has built on this truth for the last twenty-five plus years. The specialist was explaining how we as volunteers were to behave in the event of a HOSTAGE situation. First of all, we were to do basically everything asked by the inmates and not to try to be a renegade or a maverick in the situation. Then he said to rest assured that the professionals would get involved and **let them handle all communication** because they are trained on how to neutralize the threat! Then he said these words: **All communication ceases in a threat environment,** so let the professionals handle the situation.

You might be asking what that has to do with working in prayer. Simply put, EVERYTHING! Prayer is communication, and if you're going to have effective and clear communication with God and with others you simply have to learn how to remove the threat! Look to God, who is the Master Communicator. Once you begin to put together everything you've read in this book, you will find out that God is pursuing you, and His relentless, unfailing love is out to redeem and rescue you.

Many people are held HOSTAGE and you need to work in prayer and in communication to rescue them. Many are like POWs in a very real sense. They really are Prisoners of War! If you've ever seen a war movie where POWs are being rescued, sometimes they are actually reluctant to go with their rescuers! That's amazing. You would think there would be no hesitation at all. However, as a POW they have been brutalized, abused, conditioned and traumatized!

The enemy has used life and all his lies to do the very same thing to the human family ever since the fall of Adam, and like Pharoah of old, Satan has made slaves out of most people and is using them to build his kingdom or empire. He is using them to make bricks and mortar to build structures in society that serve him and his interest. The captives need to be set free. The lies need to be exposed. This book has exposed and confronted many lies, even lies that have been perpetrated through the ministry. Unfortunately, many of those bound or those who are spiritual POWs will respond just like Adam and Eve did in the Garden of Eden.

They will cover, hide, blame, and make excuses! But that won't stop love. I said,

"THAT WON'T STOP LOVE!"

Even though Adam and Eve believed a lie about God, He still made the first move and initiated communication with them. Even though they covered, hid, blamed, and made excuses, He kept the conversation going. Then thousands of years later, we heard Jesus utter these words at the Last Supper, *"Then He said to them, "With fervent desire I have desired to eat this Passover with you before I suffer;"* Luke 22:15

Why such desire? Why such passion? The last week of His life is even called THE PASSION! What is that all about? It's because He knew that once His life was laid down that all your sins would be paid for. Justice and mercy would meet at the cross and mercy would triumph! He knew that He would be raised from the dead on the third day and Holy Spirit would be released to dwell in the spirit of man once again.

After all of this He knew that **all threats would be removed** because all your sins would be removed. This is why John the Baptist cried out, "Behold the Lamb of God which takes away the sin of the world." He had to remove the sin to remove the threat. It wasn't just the forgiveness of your sins; it was the removal of them!

Jesus called himself the Door because now you can come home in your hearts to the Father and abide in His presence in newly restored innocence! It's open house in Heaven right now! This is why Colossians 1 is such an important passage for Family Mission and the Divine Reset revelation.

> *"And by the blood of his cross, everything in heaven and earth is brought back to himself— back to its original intent, restored to innocence again! Even though you were once distant from him, living in the shadows of your evil thoughts and actions, he reconnected you back to himself. He released his supernatural peace to you through the sacrifice of his own body as the sin-payment on your behalf so that you would dwell in his presence. **And now there is nothing between you and Father God, for he sees you as holy, flawless, and restored**, (THE THREAT HAS BEEN REMOVED) if indeed you continue to advance in faith, assured of a firm foundation to grow upon. Never be shaken from the hope of the Gospel you have believed*

*in. **And this is the glorious news I preach all over the \world.***"

Colossians 1:20-23 TPT

All over the world, every Tribe, Tongue, People, and Nation!

This is the place He prepared for you! A place where you could communicate freely and openly with your Father. A place where you can begin having healthy and effective communication with one another. A place where Jesus prayed from and communicated from. A place that was so fascinating that His own disciples said, "Lord, teach us to pray!" Jesus had such a reputation in prayer that Martha said these words to Him when He arrived at the tomb of Lazarus at what appeared to be too late.

*"Now Martha, as soon as she heard that Jesus was coming, went and met Him, but Mary was sitting in the house. Now Martha said to Jesus, "Lord, if You had been here, my brother would not have died. **But even now I know that whatever You ask of God, God will give You.**" Jesus said to her, "Your brother will rise again." Martha said to Him, "I know that he will rise again in the resurrection at the last day."*

*Jesus said to her, "**I am the resurrection and the life.** He who believes in Me, though he may die, he shall live. And whoever lives and believes in Me shall never die. Do you believe this?" She said to Him, "Yes, Lord, I believe that You are the Christ, the Son of God, who is to come into the world.""*

John 11:20-27

If you're going to communicate effectively with God and with others, then you need to abide in the place that Jesus prepared for you. You simply have to shift from a visitation mindset to a habitation mindset. This will take work, and this will take practice. That's right, practice. Practice His presence in every conversation. Practice His peace in every situation. Healthy communication takes work, whether that's communication with God or communication with people. It all takes practice, hard work, and dedication.

You might think that verbiage sounds like you're training for the Olympics. I used that verbiage intentionally because it will take real discipline and commitment to grow in communication with God and with others! But it will yield a reward that this life alone cannot measure or contain. It's worth all the blood, sweat, and tears.

The best place to begin with God in prayer is with what Jesus taught in Matthew 6. Everything grows out of our place with Christ and in Christ. Our place in His righteousness, authority, and purpose. Remember you need to wear that robe of righteousness He offers. You need to put on that ring of authority He gave you.

This is why you pray in Jesus' name. That's not just a sign off phrase you use. It's a stamp of authority upon every prayer and communication. You need to walk in your purpose, especially when you pray. You're not just praying to get relief! Please remind yourself of what Jesus taught regarding prayer. What did He say would be an outline or foundation for your prayers?

"And when you pray, you shall not be like the hypocrites. For they love to pray standing in the synagogues and on the corners of the streets, that they may be seen by men. Assuredly, I say to you, they have their reward. But you, when you pray, go into your room, and when you have shut your door, pray to your Father who is in the secret place; and **your Father who sees in secret will reward you openly.** *And when you pray, do not use vain repetitions as the heathen do. For they think that they will*

*be heard for their many words. "Therefore do not be like them. For **your Father knows the things you have need of before you ask Him.** In this manner, therefore, pray:*

Our Father in heaven,

Hallowed be Your name.

Your kingdom come.

Your will be done on earth as it is in heaven.

Give us this day our daily bread.

And forgive us our debts, As we forgive our debtors.

And do not lead us into temptation But deliver us from the evil one.

For Yours is the kingdom and the power and the glory forever. Amen.

"For if you forgive men their trespasses, your heavenly Father will also forgive you."

Matthew 6:5-14

Notice Jesus said God is OUR FATHER! He is talking to God the way He definitely wants you to communicate with Him. He called Him OUR FATHER. He then hallowed or honored the holy name of God. All through the Bible God is given different names. Each and every one of them are attributes expressing His goodness and holiness. So, prayer and communication with God is all based upon the integrity of His great name. It's based upon His holy and perfect character and motive.

Then Jesus tells us it's all about His Kingdom and His will being done or enforced on the earth. In other words when you work in prayer with your Father you are making deposits and downloads in the earth from heaven! Deposits and downloads in your life, home, and family. Deposits and downloads in your neighborhoods, communities, and nation! When He talks about daily bread, you can be assured that all you need is already provided. He said the Father knows what you need even before you ask, but you still need to ask not from a place where you think you're informing God of your needs.

I have found over time that the greatest hinderance or obstacle to His will is my will! That's right. My will! Your will too! I wish I could blame the devil for all the issues we see hurting humanity. But the truth is that man's will being more important than God's will has given the enemy a platform from which he does his will. Jesus lived His life every day for the Father's will and not His own. One of the most dramatic examples showing that His will was different than the Father's is in the Garden of Gethsemane. There He pleaded for another way as He said that all things are possible with His Father. Yet He ultimately submitted saying, *"Nevertheless, not My will, but Your will be done!"*

Your will, your way, your plan, as good as they may be, must always be submitted to His will, His way, and His plan. This is not something that comes easily. This is the biblical suffering that you are called to. Look at this verse in I Peter 4:1-2:

> *"Therefore, since Christ suffered for us in the flesh,* **arm yourselves also with the same mind,** *for he who has suffered in the flesh has ceased from sin, that he no longer should live the rest of his time in the flesh for the lusts of men, but* **for the will of God.** *"*

If you're going to work in prayer bringing His will in Heaven on the Earth, then you are going to have to cease from sin. Cease from doing your will and ignoring His will. Cease from doing it your way and refusing to do it His way. Cease from coming up with your plan and not seeking His plan.

Next, we see that prayer and healthy communication always have the flow of mercy in them. The third chapter of James teaches us some real lessons about communication and the flow of wisdom through healthy communication. Here's what it says:

> *"Who is wise and understanding among you? Let him show by good conduct that his works are done in the meekness of wisdom. But if you have bitter envy and self-seeking in your hearts, do not boast and lie against the truth. This wisdom does not descend from above, but is earthly, sensual, demonic. For where envy and self-seeking exist, confusion and every evil thing are there.* **But the wisdom that is from above is first pure, then peaceable, gentle, willing to yield, full of mercy and good fruits, without partiality and without hypocrisy.** *Now the fruit of righteousness is sown in peace by those who make peace."*

James 3:13-18

Simply put, wisdom coming from above is communication done right! Wisdom coming from above is communication that is seeking redemption and is seeking understanding. Wisdom coming from above is seeking to establish the will of God and the Kingdom of God in the situation. Notice the characteristics of Godly wisdom or Godly communication because this is how we need to develop and mature in our communication! Key attributes are these:

Meek or Humble

Pure

Peaceable

Gentle

Willing to listen (yield)

Full of mercy

From a good reputation

No partiality

No hypocrisy

Now you can see why I said it will take hard work, dedication, commitment, discipline, and practice. Much practice. Why? Because you have flesh, and you will have to overcome the voice of the flesh. The flesh will always entice you and try to take the conversation in a totally different direction. What are characteristics of the flesh in regard to communication of wisdom? James lists those as well.

Bitter or sharp

Envy or jealousy

Self-seeking

Self-seeking pretty well sums it all up! Are you seeking to be right or are you seeking God being right? If you're seeking God being right, then you are seeking redemption and understanding. You are seeking God's will and God's Kingdom in the situation.

Another great boost in confidence regarding prayer is **knowing that Jesus has prayed for you.** Jesus was intentional in all of His prayers. You need to be intentional in prayer as well. In John 17 He wrapped up His entire conversation recorded in John 13-16 by praying over it and into it. That's a great example right there. You should be praying over your conversations. Praying over things you said in conversation. You've already seen that your words have tremendous power. James says in chapter 2 that if you can control your tongue, you can control your whole body or your whole life.

The fact that Jesus has prayed for you should be a great encouragement because you know this about His prayers.

Remember what Martha said to Him, *"Yet even now **anything you ask God will give it you!"*** What Jesus prayed in John 17 is illustrated in John 15 when He was teaching His disciples about prayer. Here's what He said:

*"If you abide in Me, and My words abide in you, **you will ask what you desire, and it shall be done for you.** By this My Father is glorified, that you bear much fruit; so, you will be My disciples. You did not choose Me, but I chose you and appointed you that you should go and bear fruit, and that your fruit should remain, that **whatever you ask the Father in My name He may give you."***

John 15:7-8, 16

Sounds like Jesus wants you to have a reputation in prayer too. He didn't want you to simply be impressed by His prayer life. He taught you to pray and then He asked you to follow Him. One of the most important ways you follow Him, is to follow Him and His example in prayer. In John 17 listen to exactly what Jesus asked our Father and consider how it will revolutionize your prayer life.

*"I do not pray for these alone, but also for those who will believe in Me through their word; **that they all may be one, as You, Father, are in Me,***

and I in You; that they also may be one in Us, that the world may believe that You sent Me. And the glory which You gave Me I have given them, *that they may be one just as We are one: I in them, and You in Me; that they may be made perfect in one,* and that the world may know that You have sent Me and have loved them as You have loved Me."

John 17:20-23

That is one revolutionary request! That no doubt started a revolutionary war in the spirit. The devil does not want you to believe this or walk in the light of it, but it's too late. Jesus has prayed and you believe it! He wants you to live as one with your Father as He did. You still might be wondering if that's even possible. With man alone it is impossible, BUT with God all things are possible.

This is what Jesus authored and asked your Father for in prayer and this is the place He prepared for you in prayer! He intends for you to take your place in heavenly places in Christ Jesus. Remember the cry of the Moravians? The Lamb has overcome, let us follow Him. Follow Him in prayer and communication with your Father. Take your seat as Paul said in epistle to the Ephesians,

"But God, who is rich in mercy, because of His great love with which He loved us, even when we were dead in trespasses, **made us alive together with Christ** *(by grace you have been saved), and* **raised us up together, and made us sit together in the heavenly places in Christ Jesus,** *that in the ages to come He might show the exceeding riches of His grace in His kindness toward us in Christ Jesus. For by grace, you have been saved through faith, and that not of yourselves; it is the gift of God, not of works, lest anyone should boast. For we are His workmanship, created in Christ Jesus for good works, which God prepared beforehand that we should walk in them."*

Ephesians 2:4-10

This is the place He prepared for you. This is the place He prepared for you in prayer. This is the place you are to work from in prayer! In fact, Paul actually prayed for the Ephesian believers in chapter 1 and in chapter 3. You can pray these prayers today as believers.

Always prepare to receive a major supply drop when you pray them. What do I mean by that? Try to imagine troops on the ground in desperate need of supplies and then they hear the sound of distant engines of a cargo plane. A cargo plane that is bringing supplies into the region. Supplies that will be dropped in place for the ground troops! That's what I mean when you pray and work in the two Ephesian prayers. Expect a major supply drop into your life, family, and home! Here are the two prayers:

"That is why, when I heard of the solid trust you have in the Master Jesus and your outpouring of love to all the followers of Jesus, I couldn't stop thanking God for you—every time I prayed, I'd think of you and give thanks. But I do more than thank. I ask—ask the God of our Master, Jesus Christ, the God of glory—to make you intelligent and discerning in knowing him personally, your eyes focused and clear, so that you can see exactly what it is he is calling you to do, grasp the immensity of this glorious way of life he has for his followers, oh, the utter extravagance of his work in us who trust him— endless energy, boundless strength! All this energy issues from Christ: God raised him from death and set him on a throne in deep heaven, in charge of running the universe, everything from galaxies to governments, no name and no power exempt from his rule. And not just for the

time being, but forever. He is in charge of it all, has the final word on everything. At the center of all this, Christ rules the church. The church, you see, is not peripheral to the world; the world is peripheral to the church. The church is Christ's body, in which he speaks and acts, by which he fills everything with his presence."

Ephesians 1:15-23 Message Paraphrase.

"My response is to get down on my knees before the Father, this magnificent Father who parcels out all heaven and earth. I ask him to strengthen you by his Spirit—not a brute strength but a glorious inner strength—that Christ will live in you as you open the door and invite him in. And I ask him that with both feet planted firmly on love, you'll be able to take in with all followers of Jesus the extravagant dimensions of Christ's love. Reach out and experience the breadth! Test its length! Plumb the depths! Rise to the heights! Live full lives, full in the fullness of God. God can do anything, you know—far more than you could ever imagine or guess or request in your wildest dreams! He does it not by pushing us around but by working within us, his Spirit deeply and gently within us. Glory to

God in the church! Glory to God in the Messiah, in Jesus! Glory down all the generations! Glory through all millennia! Oh, yes!"

Ephesians 3:14-21 Message Paraphrase.

I chose to give you those in the Message Paraphrase. I encourage you to use other versions as well. These prayers have been a well spring and a continuous river in our family and ministry! We hope they will be in yours as well.

Finally let's look at a similar prayer that Paul prayed in Colossians chapter 1.

"For this reason we also, from the day we heard of it, have not ceased to pray and make [special] request for you, [asking] that you may be filled with the full (deep and clear) knowledge of His will in all spiritual wisdom [in comprehensive insight into the ways and purposes of God] and in understanding and discernment of spiritual things— That you may walk (live and conduct yourselves) in a manner worthy of the Lord, fully pleasing to Him and desiring to please Him in all things, bearing fruit in every good work and steadily growing and increasing in and by the knowledge of God [with fuller, deeper, and clearer insight, acquaintance, and

recognition]. [We pray] that you may be invig-orated and strengthened with all power accord-ing to the might of His glory, [to exercise] every kind of endurance and patience (perseverance and forbearance) with joy, Giving thanks to the Father, Who has qualified and made us fit to share the portion which is the inheritance of the saints (God's holy people) in the Light. [The Father] has delivered and drawn us to Himself out of the control and the dominion of dark-ness and has transferred us into the kingdom of the Son of His love, In Whom we have our redemption through His blood, [which means] the forgiveness of our sins."

Colossians 1:9-14 AMPC.

Paul gives further vital teaching in the letter to the Romans about prayer with the help of Holy Spirit!

"Likewise the Spirit also helps in our weakness-es. For we do not know what we should pray for as we ought, but the Spirit Himself makes intercession for us with groanings which can-not be uttered (in articulate speech on trans-lation says) Now He who searches the hearts knows what the mind of the Spirit is, because

*He makes intercession for the saints according
to the will of God. And we know that all things
work together for good to those who love God,
to those who are the called according to His
purpose."*

Romans 8:26-28

First of all, I need to clarify something here in the NKJV. This phrase "according to the will of God" is a powerful truth when you consider praying with the help of the Holy Spirit. These utterances and groanings are what the Bible refers to as praying in other tongues, yet in the marginal reference of any King James Bible, you will see the words "the will of" are italicized. This means they were added by translators in hopes of clarification. Well, it's true that when you pray in the Spirit or with the help of the Holy Spirit you are praying "according to the will of God."

But let's remove those couple of italicized words and see what it says. He makes intercession for the saints **according to God!** Wow, now that's even more potent. When you pray in the Spirit and in other tongues you are praying ACCORDING TO GOD! Not just His will, but His power, and His vantage point! Not just His will, but His motive and His patience! Here's what Paul said to the Corinthians about praying in other tongues.

*"Pursue love, and desire spiritual gifts, but especially that you may prophesy. For **he who speaks in a tongue** does not speak to men but **to God,** for no one understands him; **however, in the spirit he speaks mysteries. He who speaks in a tongue edifies himself,** but he who prophesies edifies the church. Therefore, let him who speaks in a tongue **pray that he may interpret.** For if I pray in a tongue, **my spirit prays,** but my understanding is unfruitful. What is the conclusion then? **I will pray with the spirit, and I will also pray with the understanding.** I will sing with the spirit, and I will also sing with the understanding.*

I Corinthians 14:1-2, 4, 13-15

Certain portions are made bold here for emphasis to clearly see the benefits Paul lines out regarding prayer in the Spirit or in other tongues. Here are a few of these verses in the Amplified Classic Version:

"For one who speaks in an [unknown] tongue speaks not to men but to God, for no one understands or catches his meaning, because in the

*[Holy] Spirit **he utters secret truths and hidden things [not obvious to the understanding].** He who speaks in a [strange] tongue **edifies and improves himself,** but he who prophesies [interpreting the divine will and purpose and teaching with inspiration] edifies and improves the church and promotes growth [in Christian wisdom, piety, holiness, and happiness]. **For if I pray in an [unknown] tongue, my spirit [by the Holy Spirit within me] prays,** but my mind is unproductive [it bears no fruit and helps nobody]. Then what am I to do? **I will pray with my spirit [by the Holy Spirit that is within me], but I will also pray [intelligently] with my mind and understanding;** I will sing with my spirit [by the Holy Spirit that is within me], but I will sing [intelligently] with my mind and understanding also."*

1 Corinthians 14:2, 4, 14-15 AMPC

If we're going to work in prayer to our full potential, then we certainly cannot leave out Paul's teaching on prayer found in Ephesians 6.

"Finally, my brethren, be strong in the Lord and in the power of His might. Put on the whole

*armor of God, **that you may be able to stand against the wiles of the devil.** For we do not wrestle against flesh and blood, but against principalities, against powers, against the rulers of the darkness of this age, against spiritual hosts of wickedness in the heavenly places. Therefore, take up **the whole armor of God,** that you may be able to withstand in the evil day, and having done all, to stand. Stand therefore, having girded your waist with **truth**, having put on the breastplate of **righteousness**, and having shod your feet with the preparation of the **Gospel of peace;** above all, taking the shield of **Faith** with which, you will be able to quench all the fiery darts of the wicked one. And take the helmet of **salvation**, and the sword of the Spirit, which is **the word of God, praying always with all prayer** and supplication **in the Spirit, being watchful** to this end with all perseverance and supplication for all the saints—"*

Ephesians 6:10-18

Here's a really important thing to remember when working with God in prayer. You are not working against any mighty power of the devil in your life or other people's lives. Jesus stripped the devil of his power and his authority! Jesus said we would TRAMPLE over all the power of the enemy. What you are working against is mostly the enemy's WILES and his SCHEMES. That's an important shift to make in our thinking and our perspective! Remember, Paul said to be strong in the Lord. In other words, **be strong in the place you've been given in prayer!**

This means true spiritual warfare and working with God in prayer will many times be simply removing, uprooting, and exposing lies, and then replacing them with the truth. Enforcing and replacing truth where lies have previously influenced you. Let me say that again. It's many times going to be removing, uprooting, or exposing lies, and then replacing them or enforcing truth in that area.

Notice what Paul said would be accomplished when he gave you the soldier's armor analogy. In his analogy he talked about a belt, a breastplate, shoes, a shield, a helmet, and a sword. The analogy is indeed a powerful thing. It has many implications for sure. Yet you cannot elevate the analogy above the eternal things they represent. Here is a list in order of all the things Paul talks about in his soldier analogy:

Truth

Righteousness

The Gospel of Peace

Faith

Working in Prayer

Salvation

The Word of God

Then Paul applies it all to
WORKING IN PRAYER!

All manner of prayer In the Spirit

Being watchful in supplication and perseverance

Notice again what he said in verse 18. **"Praying always with all prayer** and supplication **in the Spirit, being watchful** to this end with all perseverance and supplication for all the saints—"** Praying always and praying with all manner of prayer and supplication (requests). Then he said to do it all in the Spirit and he said to be watchful. He also said that you were going to need perseverance to pray for all the saints.

This is some incredible instruction and guidance in prayer. I especially want to highlight the phrase to BE WATCHFUL. This gives you the imagery of being a watchman on the wall watching over the city! Being alert and ready in prayer. If you're going to work in prayer like Jesus did and like you're called to, then you will need to be alert and ready, not lazy and not asleep on your watch! Not just praying on a schedule alone.

We need to watch over our marriages in prayer.

We need to watch over our children in prayer.

We need to watch over our families in prayer.

We need to watch over the church in prayer.

We need to watch over our communities in prayer.

We need to watch over our nation in prayer.

Here's some further instructions along this line taken from Paul's instructions to the Colossians in chapter 4:2. He said, *"Be **earnest** and **unwearied** and **steadfast** in your prayer [life], being [both] alert and intent in [your praying] **with thanksgiving.**" AMPC.*

One version says to watch over your prayers with thanksgiving! This simply means you're going to have to be intentional to record what you are praying over and praying about. You and I can forget way too easily. We all have flesh and can forget. It's so important to develop some system of recording things that people ask you to pray about. First, so you can remember to pray, and then so you can watch over them after you've prayed about it. You may be saying that seems like a lot of work! There's a reason we called this chapter **working in prayer** because it is work. It's a privileged work. Just like Adam kept watch over the Garden, you need to keep watch over your garden. The garden of your life, family, and home. **You need to be earnest, unwearied, steadfast, and thankful in your prayers.**

Here's a couple things John said about prayer that are truly helpful as well:

> *"For if our heart condemns us, God is greater than our heart, and knows all things. Beloved, if our heart does not condemn us, we have confidence toward God. And **whatever we ask we receive from Him,** because we keep His commandments and do those things that are pleasing in His sight."*

> **I John 3:20-22**

Because of the blood of Jesus, you can confess your sins and be cleansed from all unrighteousness (I John 1:9). God is greater than your heart and He has provided you with a robe of righteousness that He expects you to wear and not take off! Never pray without your robe, ring and sandals on!

> *"Now this is the confidence that we have in Him, that if we ask anything according to His will, **He hears us. And if we know that He***

hears us, whatever we ask, we know that we have the petitions that we have asked of Him."

I John 5:14-15

If He hears you, then you definitely need to be continually flowing in thanksgiving in the realm of prayer. This will take work, and this will take practice, but Holy Spirit will train you and grace you to work in prayer effectively. Remember, there will be no Divine Reset without working in prayer, without healthy communication! Healthy communication will take work! You must work at having truly intimate communication with Him and with each other. You must work to remove the threat in your home and family. Just like your Father removed the threat on the cross.

In closing. here are six very important keys that you can use to unlock your destiny and your family's destiny! They are found in these passages in Romans chapter 8.

*"For I consider that the sufferings of this present time are not worthy to be compared with the glory which shall be revealed in us. For the earnest expectation of the creation eagerly waits for **the revealing of the sons of God.** (The Family of God) For the creation was subjected to futility, not willingly, but because of Him*

*who subjected it in hope, because the creation itself also will be delivered from the bondage of corruption into **the glorious liberty of the children of God. (The Family of God)***

Romans 8:18-21

*And we know that all things work together for good to those who love God, to those who are the called according to **His purpose**. For whom He **foreknew**, He also **predestined** to be conformed to the image of His Son, that He might be the firstborn among many brethren. Moreover, whom He predestined, these He also **called**; whom He called, these He also **justi-fied**; and whom He justified, these He also **glo-rified**. What then shall we say to these things? If God is for us, who can be against us? He who did not spare His own Son, but delivered Him up for us all, how shall He not with Him also freely give us all things?"*

Romans 8:28-32

1. His Purpose: Throughout the ages to come we will work with Him.

2. Foreknowledge: This is what God knows about your life.

3. Predestination: This is what God has prepared and planned for your life.

4. Justified: Sin has been removed from your life by the blood and body of Jesus.

5. Called: He is pursuing you and speaking to you from your future and the fulfilled place you have in Christ Jesus.

6. Glorified: Holy Spirit lives in your spirit and is in you now.

**These 6 truths affect the place
He prepared for us in prayer.**

**Based on these, here are 6 important
guidelines you can use in prayer.**

1. Always work with His purpose in prayer. Not your purpose and motive, but His.

2. Always work from a place that recognizes and accesses the foreknowledge of God. It is available and it is accessible!

3. Always work with the destination He's prepared in mind. He has a blueprint. You must build according to His blueprint.

4. Always work from a place of righteousness. Make sure you wear the robe, ring, and shoes He put on you when you came home - your redeemed value, identity, and purpose.

5. Always remember He's the one leading the relationship. He leads in your worship. He leads in your intimacy, agreement, and partnership. So, He leads as you work in prayer as well.

6. Always yield to the glory of God in your life as you work in prayer. You're not praying in the flesh. You're praying in and with the Holy Spirit. You're working in the glory of God. You're praying according to God!

Closing Thoughts...

Every Tribe, Tongue, People and Nation deserves a chance to be born again and experience a Divine Reset. Everyone should be given a chance to come home in their heart to OUR FATHER. Everyone's destiny is a living and vital part of His legacy.

Every mountain of influence or cultural territory needs to be flooded with the power and love of Christ. They need to see someone alive IN CHRIST wearing the robe of righteousness, the ring of authority and the shoes of divine purpose!

Let's live and work in prayer to bring the Kingdom of God into

Family, Faith, Media, Government, Commerce, Education and Entertainment/Arts.

Let's get to work …

Appendix 1

Being Born-Again and Being Baptized in the Holy Spirit

It's Time to Move into Your Mansion

Coming home in your heart all begins with being born-again! Jesus said you **must** be born-again! (John 3:3) He also said, "you cannot even see or understand the Kingdom of God until you're born again." In other words, you need to be re-Fathered. Everyone on the Earth is a descendant of a fallen Adam and the only way to change families is through death and a resurrection! That's exactly right! Please let me explain. Jesus, by faith, laid His life down and became what He did not deserve. (II Corinthians 5:21) You also can, by faith, lay your life down and become what you do not deserve! He was rejected, you are accepted. He was punished, you are justified. He identified with your sinfulness so you could identify with His righteousness! Water baptism is the perfect witness to the new birth experience. You actually come alive again into a new family tree and it's a tree of righteousness: the planting of the Lord. (Isaiah 61:3) The Bible calls us in II Corinthians 5:17 a new creation.

Christians are actually new creations that have never existed before until Christ died and rose from the dead and sent the Holy Spirit. You're in a new family tree! Jesus Is the Root.

II Corinthians 5:17 says, "that all things pass away and behold all things have become new!" As Christians, the new birth experience actually engrafted us into Christ. One person said it this way, we've been "In-Christed!" As Christians we are now in the vine Jesus spoke of in John 15:1-17. A new vine means a new family! A new vine that's rooted in His divine love. The Greek word for God's love is *agape*. Now we all can have a type A personality! Type Agape!

In John 15:7 Jesus said, "If we abide or remain, we will ask for what we desire, and it shall be done for us." The world needs to see someone who really knows God personally as their Father. This is NOT just knowing about Him! The world needs to see someone who's in real communication with God. **There is a HUGE difference between someone who knows about God and someone who really knows God intimately!**

The world needs to see someone who knows God's voice and who gets their prayers answered. This is not just about the accumulation of selfish desires through prayer.

This is about getting His will in Heaven accomplished in the Earth through prayer.

Jesus had a reputation in prayer. We as Christians, also can have a reputation in prayer! Jesus said in John 14:12 that He was counting on us doing the very same works that He did. He revealed that it wasn't Him doing the works, but the Father in Him. That's telling us that the works of Jesus flowed out of His communication and communion with the Father.

Our works will also flow out of our communication and communion with the Heavenly Father! Remember, this is **the place** He prepared for you!

Jesus said that He was just doing what He saw His Father do and He simply said what His Father gave Him to say. Do you hear the emphasis He placed on His relationship with the Father? Everything we do with church and the Bible or in prayer must be focused on an intimate relationship and not systems, formulas, and programs!

Jesus by the way, never had any lack in His life! Jesus was not poor! He gave to the poor. How many poor people do you know who have a treasurer? A treasurer who was constantly stealing from Him by the way! The Bible says God gives us richly all things to enjoy. It's okay to have anything you enjoy. We just need to make sure the things we enjoy are not getting in the way of our obedience to His instructions and directions in our lives.

Perhaps you want to be born-again or you're not sure if you are born-again. Believing in Jesus is not enough. Going to church is not enough. Jesus said, "You must be born-again" (John 3:3). I would like to lead you in a prayer, so you can, by faith, lay your self-centered life, a life you were never intended to live, down and receive by faith the divine seed of the life of God (I Peter 1:22,23). The seed of a Love centered life, the one you were intended and destined to live! So, if there's any uncertainty in your heart or if you simply want to repent and reconsecrate, please pray these words with sincere faith! Open your heart wide and take a deep breath as you pray … and receive the Holy Spirit!

Heavenly Father thank you for sending Jesus on a Mission of Love. Thank you for never losing sight of who I was even when I was living life in the darkness. Thank you for paying the price my sins required. Thank you for being a just and holy God! Thank you for raising Jesus from the dead for the remission and removal of my sins. Thank you for the cleansing blood of Jesus. Thank you, Jesus, for taking

by faith all my sin and all its penalty which you did not deserve so that I might by faith lay hold of Your life and all its fullness which I don't deserve.

By faith I lay down my selfish, self-centered, sinful life- a life I was never created to live. By faith I take the seed of truth and love, the divine seed of God in my heart that I might be born again! By faith I receive the presence and power of Holy Spirit to overshadow me like He did Mary when she conceived Christ Himself. By faith I receive the seed of Christ in the womb of my spirit right now! By faith I take hold of the power of a resurrected life, the power of a brand-new life in Christ Jesus!

I declare old things have passed away and behold all things have become new and all things are of God. I have been crucified with Christ; it is no longer I who live, but Christ lives in me; and the life which I now live in the flesh I live by the faith of the Son of God, who loved me and gave Himself for me. I will NOT resist the grace of God, but I receive it in abundance right NOW as I am engrafted into Christ.

Christ who is the vine of life and the vine of love.

Thank you, Holy Spirit, for doing this work right NOW! Glory to God and thank You Jesus! Thank you, Lord, for preparing this amazing place for me!

If you prayed this prayer, welcome to the Family of God. Welcome into the Family Mission. We encourage you to get water baptized and get in a good, Bible-based assembly of believers. If you need help finding one you can contact us at **spellmanministries@gmail.com.**

Next, I want to encourage you to receive the baptism in the Holy Spirit and fire! John the Baptist said in Luke 3:16 that Jesus would baptize with the Holy Spirit and fire! One of the MANY blessed results of this baptism is that you will be able to speak in other tongues, tongues of fire. According to Jesus in John 7:37,38, RIVERS of living water will begin flowing in your life. In the Book of Acts this is the promise of the Father Jesus was speaking about. Jesus is God's gift to the world. The Holy Spirit is God's gift to the church. Jesus said it this way in Acts 1:8 "... but you shall receive power when the Holy Spirit has come upon you; and you shall be witnesses to Me in Jerusalem, and in all Judea and Samaria, and to the end of the earth."

This book in your hand is all about us being that witness! A witness to the truth and a witness to the love of God. Being a witness means our lives provide evidence that Jesus is alive, and God sent Him and raised Him from the dead. We are to be living proof!

Jesus breathed on His disciples in John 20:22 and they were born-again. That's what you just experienced. This is an exact parallel of Genesis 2:7 where God breathed into the nostrils of Adam, and he came alive!

The outpouring of the Holy Spirit in Acts 2:1-4 is an additional experience with the Holy Spirit! Jesus wanted us filled with the Holy Spirit and fire. When we are born again, we become the temple of the Holy Spirit, but Jesus said His followers needed this added experience with the Holy Spirit and fire. At the end of the Gospels, Jesus commanded His disciples to go, but He also said for them to wait on the baptism of the Holy Spirit and fire before they were to go!

I say we do just what He says, how about you? If you've never been baptized with the Holy Spirit and fire with the evidence of speaking in other tongues, let me lead you in a prayer to receive this baptism! Please don't be afraid of the fire of God. The Bible says our God is a consuming fire. He simply wants you to be consumed in love like Him! In Luke 11:11-13 Jesus said that if an earthly father would give you what you needed and asked for how much more will the Heavenly Father give the Holy Spirit to them that ask Him! I hope you will open your heart and pray this prayer with me now.

Jesus, thank you for the promise of the Father! I know you said that if a child asked his father for a piece of bread, he wouldn't give the child a stone. How much more you said will the Heavenly Father give the Holy Spirit to them who ask.

I am asking you right now for the fullness and fire of the Holy Spirit. I want to be baptized and immersed in the Holy Spirit and fire! I want to speak in other tongues. I want tongues of fire right now in the name of Jesus. I want a life that burns for Jesus Christ and His eternal Kingdom! I believe I receive right now in the name of Jesus!

Okay ... Let those rivers of living water bubble up and gush forth out of your belly right now. Not out of your head, but out of your belly! God will not make you speak. You give Him sound and He shapes the utterance. Let it go and let it flow right now in Jesus' name!

If you prayed either of these prayers or have any questions, please let our ministry know by contacting us at **spellmanministries@gmail.com**. There are also resources available for you at **spellmanministries.org.** You can also subscribe to our Facebook page and YouTube channel for more resources. Simply find us at Spellman Ministries. All of us at Family Mission love you and are praying for you.

Reviving the Mission of Love,

Mark, Kimberly, Samuel, and Daniel Spellman